IF

If you can keep your head when all about you
Are losing theirs and blaming it on you,
If you can trust yourself when all men doubt you
But make allowance for their doubting too,
If you can wait and not be tired by waiting,
Or being lied about, don't deal in lies,
Or being hated, don't give way to hating,
And yet don't look too good, nor talk too wise:

If you can dream—and not make dreams your master,
If you can think—and not make thoughts your aim;
If you can meet with Triumph and Disaster
And treat those two impostors just the same;
If you can bear to hear the truth you've spoken
Twisted by knaves to make a trap for fools,
Or watch the things you gave your life to, broken,
And stoop and build 'em up with worn-out tools:

If you can make one heap of all your winnings
And risk it all on one turn of pitch-and-toss,
And lose, and start again at your beginnings
And never breath a word about your loss;
If you can force your heart and nerve and sinew
To serve your turn long after they are gone,
And so hold on when there is nothing in you
Except the Will which says to them: "Hold on!"

If you can talk with crowds and keep your virtue,
Or walk with kings—nor lose the common touch,
If neither foes nor loving friends can hurt you;
If all men count with you, but none too much,
If you can fill the unforgiving minute
With sixty seconds' worth of distance run,
Yours is the Earth and everything that's in it,
And—which is more—you'll be a Man, my son!

– **Rudyard Kipling**

Raising Athletic Stars

How to Put Integrity and Character Development Back in Play

By Theodore Dance
With Elizabeth Latrobe Place

First Books Publishing Company
502 West 8th. Street
Erie, Pa. 16502
877-454-4620
firstbooks@aol.com
www.firstbooks.net

Printed in the United States of America
10 9 8 7 6 5 4 3 2 1

Library of Congress Control Number: 2005909782

Paperback ISBN: 0-615-12735-5
Hardcover ISBN: 0-9776638-0-9

Book cover and interior design by: Bookcovers.com

TABLE OF CONTENTS

DEDICATION

I would first like to thank God for the time and opportunity to write this book and share it with readers. In addition, I would like to thank my mother, who made me the man I am today. When I was a single parent raising two children, she played a large role helping me with their upbringing. Last, but not least, I would like to thank my sons. None of this would have been possible without their hard work, dedication, vision, and tolerance as I constantly pushed them beyond their limits. Timmy and Tommy, I am so proud of you both.

Where there is no vision, people perish.
~ Proverbs 29.18

My Mother, Marva Simmons

INTRODUCTION

**A ship in the harbor is safe. But that is not
what ships are for.**
~ Unknown

I am the proud father of two young men who both developed into outstanding athletes and went on to Division I-A college scholarships. I have written this book in response to the many questions I've received over the years regarding my sons' athletic successes. It is my intention to help parents learn how to support their children's efforts to become outstanding athletes. More importantly, my book is about instilling integrity and character in every young man and woman. Whether your children go on to pursue a college scholarship or just become lifelong recreational athletes, sports can help them succeed in life.

As an athlete myself, I sincerely appreciated the role sports played in my life. As a young athlete, I received statewide recognition in football and that experience has had a positive impact throughout my lifetime. From the time my sons could walk, I decided that they too could benefit from all the gifts that come from athletic pursuits. Discipline, mental and physical strength and financial opportunity can all come from pursuing sports on a serious level.

Our story gains a universal appeal with my sons' common challenge: neither displayed any natural athletic ability as children. Lack of coordination discouraged them both. I still tease them about their awkward beginnings. Nevertheless, through hard work and dedication, they blossomed into disciplined athletes and both went on to break records, win state championships and earn college scholarships.

My own definition of an athletic star is embodied in my sons. I have interviewed many outstanding sports professionals for this book and we all agree on certain attributes. An athletic star is someone who:

- Works to develop extraordinary talent
- Tries their best
- Is knowledgeable about their sport
- Is a good team player and a good sport
- Respects teammates, competitors, umpires, coaches and fans
- Never uses drugs, performance enhancing or otherwise
- Loves their sport
- Never cheats
- Gives back to their sport and to their community
- Never gives up

HOW DO YOU DEFINE AN ATHLETIC STAR?

I am proud to say that my sons are athletic stars; in part because they know that winning is not everything. I taught my boys to have balance in their lives, and I taught them that they must suffer set backs and disappointments in order to learn and grow. They had to lose and fall short in order to develop as players, students, and human beings. Losing is as significant as winning when it comes to development in the student-athlete.

While I taught them to have a winning attitude, I also taught them not to have a win-at-any-cost attitude. That mindset sacrifices integrity, trust, relationships, careers, and even marriages. As many professional athletes have proven, cheaters never win. Nowhere was it better illustrated than in the 2005 Congressional Baseball hearings on steroid use. The panel of so-called star baseball players either refused to discuss steroid use or bragged about it. It was a disgusting display of greed and selfishness. These men humiliated themselves in their pursuit of winning.

How can someone be considered an athletic star if he cheats and then denies or refuses to discuss his mistakes? We need to work together to put an end to the cheating and violent behavior that we have come to witness in organized sports. We can win this fight. I believe that as parents our battlefield is on Little League lots, peewee hockey rinks, tennis courts and balance beams. We must make sure that we don't raise student-athletes who are willing to win at any cost and become adults who cheat to win.

Even though I have enjoyed the success of my sons on the playing field, I am constantly reminding them that what I am most proud of is the integrity and character they possess. It is their honesty, humbling spirit and academic achievements that mean the most. When parents, coaches and teachers tell me how well mannered my sons are, that is what I am most proud of. That is what it was really about for me, raising good sons with great character.

Fred Engh, President of the **National Alliance for Youth Sports**, said in 2005 that approximately 70 percent of children who compete in organized sports quit by age 13. He attributes this to the pressure and unpleasantness that coaches and parents are imposing on them. Fred says, "If it's not fun, then kids are not going to want to participate." I agree with him. We can encourage, support and inspire our student-athletes without pushing them over the edge.

I hope that as a responsible parent you will not only raise a star athlete with character, but you will help other parents realize the importance of their roles. We can all pull together to help a new generation of young people grow up to be happy, healthy adults who value achievement in athletics and all aspects of life.

I had the good fortune to have Tony Dungy, Head Coach of the Indianapolis Colts give us some thoughts for this book. I asked him what role sports played in raising his children and this is what he had to say.

NFL Head Coach Tony Dungy, Indianapolis Colts

I've been in sports all my life and it teaches you a lot of things, teamwork, working towards a common goal and that you aren't always going to win no matter how hard you work at it. Those are some things I've tried to get across to my kids. You have to be good family members but no matter how you work, things may not always go your way. You have to stick to what you believe in and continue to try to do your best. I think those things have really helped my kids growing up.

Try not to become a man of success but rather to become a man of value.
~ Albert Einstein

Tommy Dance 2004 State Champion, High School Track

Timmy Dance, 1992 Youth Hockey

CHAPTER ONE

LEARNING

The will to win is important, but the will to prepare is vital.
~Joe Paterno

Imagine how much farther your children will go in life, if you instill in them a love of learning. If your kids want to learn, life will be an adventure, not a chore. Every goal that your child sets during their lifetime will require a first step and a commitment to learning. Sports are an excellent way to get your child started down that path.

Paint a big picture for your young athletes. They will start off without knowledge or skills but they can develop into a great athlete over time. Take a pee wee hockey player for example. He or she will start off with nothing, first learning the basic rules and skills, barely able to skate to the end of the rink. But it's the same game of hockey that Wayne Gretsky played. The difference between them lies in their level of skill, knowledge, commitment and dedication. Every great athlete started with a first pass, or swing or hurdle cleared and then progressed by wanting to learn how to do it better. After all, Michael Jordon wasn't born shooting hoops. Every athlete has to begin somewhere and I believe that it starts with a love of learning and a desire to succeed.

Raising an athletic star is not about pushing young athletes to win at any cost, it's about teaching them to be good competitors who respect their sport. When I think about children looking up to great athletes, I'm sad for today's young baseball players. Who are their heroes? Too many of the big hitters have tarnished the game with steroid-induced records. Our children shouldn't be looking up to cheaters. We should be teaching our kids to value fair play and sportsmanship. And that's where you come in; and that's why I wrote this book.

Make It Fun

It will take time and experimentation for your child to latch on to a specific sport. Right from the start, you should put the focus on fun and learning, not the gold medal twenty years in the future. It's not the 'win' in the distance that is important but all the lessons learned on the journey to winning that will help them grow into well adjusted adults. It's time to get back to basics and teach our kids that what is important in sports, is not whether you win or lose but how you play the game.

You will read many personal stories in this book from student and professional athletes and each one credits a parent or a coach for inspiring them to learn and succeed in their sport. I encourage you to be that person in a child's life.

Teaching Respect

The very first thing you need to teach your children is to respect the rules of a sport. Safety and sportsmanship should be taught before skills training. Kids will have more fun playing a game if they play by the rules and no amount of skill or athleticism will replace basic respect for the coach and the referee. When a basketball player learns not to travel or a pee wee hockey player learns not to hit his opponent with the hockey stick, they are learning a much bigger lesson; to respect authority. Too often I see cheating and poor behavior overlooked in organized youth sports, in favor of winning. When you allow children to cheat or talk back to a referee, you are setting a dangerous precedent for them, on and off the playing field. Ask yourself, how many professional athletes have cheated to win, disappointing millions of fans? Beyond that, how many business executives have destroyed companies and lives, because they didn't follow the rules? When I see a parent letting a child get away with bad behavior or cheating, I can't help but wonder what kind of adult they will become. Clearly, lessons learned on the playing field affect children throughout their lives.

routes was an important basic skill for them to learn. If they made mistakes or didn't show a good effort, I'd demonstrate the right way and we would work on it until they got it right. I never pointed out the mistakes or yelled at them; I just encouraged them to do it the right way and praised them for improving. Because children have limited attention spans, I always found it best to spend a little time each day on a skill rather than hours at a time.

TIPS FOR TEACHING YOUNG CHILDREN

- Speak in a calm voice – don't yell
- Have eye contact whenever possible
- Ask them to repeat what you say
- State your message in different ways – paint a verbal picture
- Use visual aids
- Demonstrate and give examples
- When correcting – use positive language and praise
- Focus on behaviors and skills – not personalities
- Show respect and demand respect in return

START YOUNG

Regardless of age, young athletes should try many sports. Keep in mind however; they should start to focus on a specific sport as soon as possible. It's essential that young children enjoy themselves while they learn. If they experience a lot of disappointment or feel inadequate, they may not want to return for another season. Make sure they look forward to the next steps and new seasons ahead.

Tommy Dance: Division I College Football Player

When I was little, I used to watch my father and older brother throw the football around, and I wanted to learn so badly. They used to have so much fun. I couldn't wait to get a football in my hands.

Remember to let your kids be kids and set aside time for them to learn healthy social skills. Raising athletic stars means raising respectful young men and women who enjoy themselves. Children with great attitudes, who learn right from wrong, will carry those lessons onto the playing field, setting them apart from their peers. Respect for authority and fellow athletes, kindness, helpfulness, mental focus and purpose are essential. A healthy moral fiber and spiritual foundation will sustain them throughout their lifetime. Help your child seek greatness but also goodness.

Learn to Avoid the Biggest Mistake

The biggest mistake a parent can make is teaching a young child that winning is everything. This message is false and destructive and it bombards us each day. I heard a sports broadcaster practically dismiss a pro baseball player's use of steroids, saying "How can you argue with the guy, if he was helping his team win?" As parents looking to instill character and integrity into our young athletes, we have to take every opportunity to fight that win-at-any-cost mentality. You can counteract it by encouraging your child to focus on playing the game, on the competition and on sportsmanship.

Skier Bode Miller has been hounded for returning home from the 2006 Winter Olympics without a medal. While his behavior has been questionable, I like the message that he has for young athletes. Bode believes that young athletes are giving up on sports because they think that they will never win a gold medal or get to the top. Win or lose, Bode loves to ski and he thinks that kids should start feeling the same way about their own sport. I think that we've gotten to a point where there is no longer value in the silver or bronze medal. We have to turn it around and celebrate any achievement in sports.

Autistic high school basketball manager Jason McElwain was put into a basketball game for the very first time in his life and scored 20 points in four minutes. He has been an inspiration to athletes everywhere and received a visit from the President and a slew of Hollywood producers looking to write his story. He didn't win a gold medal; he just thrilled us all with his effort and enthusiasm.

Let's get back to the place where we value the thrill of competition in favor of the final score.

Sam Maniar, Ph.D. Sport Psychologist for Optimal Performance Consulting

The most important thing to remember when working with young children is to keep it fun. They are not getting involved in sports to become millionaires or even to get a college scholarship--they are playing sports because it's fun. Too often, parents become overly involved in the child's athletic performance and in doing so they take away all the fun.

When teaching young athletes (e.g., 7-9 year-olds) skills, it is also important to break things down into small, manageable steps. Give them one goal to work on at a time. Once they have mastered this, add a second, and so on. Additionally, young children thrive on praise. Rather than correcting something done wrong, it is often more powerful to wait and catch them doing something right. When this happens, give them a lot of praise, and they will remember the correct way much easier than if you are continuously correcting them.

Young children also have short attention spans, so keep practice lengths limited to the same amount of time they will play in competition. For example, if the team will play two, 25-minute halves, then keep practice limited to 50 minutes. Start with skill development one-on-one and gradually move to game situations.

Put children in many different situations and positions, but always set them up for success. This will give them more chances to learn how to overcome obstacles and to persevere. Young children should never be put in impossible situations in order to "build character."

Finally, find ways to make drills more fun and exciting, and be ready to move onto something new when the drills are no longer fun. Also, give children time to play without any feedback. That being said, parents and coaches should not even worry about mental toughness when it comes to 7-9 year-olds. They're too young to even consider building such skills.

Doing the right thing when no one is looking is how I define integrity in an athlete. One of my favorite quotes is: "The vision of a champion is someone who is bent over, drenched in sweat, at the point of exhaustion when no one else is watching." (Anson Dorrance, head women's soccer coach, University of North Carolina). In order for children to understand this, it must be taught at home. And because children learn a lot from observation, parents and coaches must be willing to "do the right thing" or choose the harder right over the easier wrong in all aspects of their lives. Additionally, children must be shown the rewards that will come from putting in the hard work. As far as things parents and coaches can do, it can be as simple as asking the child on a daily basis: "What did you do to make yourself a better _____ (person, athlete, student, member of society) today?"

It Starts At Home

Before your children are ever exposed to a team or a coach, teach them discipline. Even young children should get in the habit of attending scheduled practices and setting aside additional time at home to work on skills. Try to create an atmosphere at home where you can practice skills and exercise together. No matter what sport you are practicing with your kids, focus on the great single moments like the one great shot on the tennis court and the ball knocked over the fence. I believe that kids will want to practice if they find real enjoyment in improving their skills.

Encouraging regular exercise and participation sends a message to stick with a sport. Once committed to a sport, they should not be allowed to quit before the end of a season or until they have proven that they have given it their all.

Search, and you will find; knock, and the door will be opened to you.
~ Luke 11:10

WHICH SPORT?

Most children get started in a sport because of a parent's or relative's interest or through a school or community program. When your child is young, you can broaden your thinking about different

---

ARCHERY

This sport has prehistoric roots. It simply involves shooting an arrow at a target. Both males and females compete. Children as young as 7 participate in the sport, and there is no age limit. Competition goes from junior through adult world championships.

Equipment: Bows, arrows, arrow heads and targets

Learn more: http://www.usarchery.org

BADMINTON

This co-ed racket sport is played in backyards and competitively in junior high school, high school, college, and adult international competitions.

Equipment: Badminton racket, birdie, tennis shoes, badminton court

Learn more: http://www.usabadminton.org

BASEBALL

America's pastime is played by boys and girls as young as 7 in Little League-type programs. Professional baseball players are some of the highest paid athletes.

Equipment: Baseball cleats, bat, ball, baseball glove, helmet, protective gear, sandlot or stadium baseball field.

Learn more: http://www.juniorbaseball.com

BASKETBALL

Invented by Dr. Luther Halsey Gulick, Jr., the superintendent of physical education at the international YMCA Training School during the summer session of 1891. This international game was meant to provide indoor physical activity during winter months. Basketball is played by men and women as young as age 5 in grade schools through high school, college, professional and international championships.

Equipment: Sneakers, basketball, basketball net and/or court

Learn more:
http://www.internationalbasketball.com/usa.html

BOWLING

This indoor sport can be traced back to the year 1366 in England. It is popular for both men and women, recreationally and competitively, in high school, college and professional programs.

Equipment: Bowling ball, bowling shoes and bowling alley - all of which can be rented for little money.

Learn more: http://www.bowl.com

CROSS COUNTRY

This sport for men and women involves long distance running that usually takes place over rough terrain. This is a high school, college and world championship sport and is one of the purest and least expensive of all sports.

Equipment: Running shoes

Learn more: http://www.usatf.org

DIVING

This sport often starts with children at play but can develop for men and women into a college and Olympic endeavor. While the equipment requirements are minimal, pool and diving board time may require long distance driving and early morning practice hours.

Equipment: Bathing suit, pool, diving board

Learn more:
http://library.thinkquest.org/27480/diving.html

EQUESTRIAN

This involves a rider on a horse negotiating a rough terrain course or a choreographed routine in a riding ring. High-level competition can last well into a person's 50's or 60's. It can be very expensive depending on ownership and travel to events or made economical through rental of horse and equipment.

Equipment: Horse, tack, riding boots and apparel, hard hat, riding ring or course

Learn more: http://www.usef.org

FENCING

Fencing as a modern sport is approximately 90 years old. This sport for men and women involves two opponents, each with a sword-like weapon. Most of the actual competition in fencing takes place in fencing tournaments, ranging from club-run tournaments to the Olympics. The competition has no age limit.

Equipment: Mask and weapon – a saber, epee or foil

Learn more: http://www.usfencing.org

FIELD HOCKEY

This sport, played primarily by females, involves two teams brandishing J- shaped sticks while hitting a ball on the ground towards the opponent's goal. Women's field hockey became popular after the Moscow Olympics in 1980. Field hockey is a college, professional, and international sport.

Equipment: Protective gear, ball, stick, playing field

Learn more: http://www.usfieldhockey.com

FOOTBALL

Played by boys and men, if not America's favorite sport, it is surely number two. Football is played from grade school to high school, college, and professional leagues and is an international sport.

Equipment: Helmet, mouthpiece, cleats and extensive protective gear, football and playing field

Learn more: http://www.popwarner.com

GOLF

This sport, which originated in Scotland, is played by men and women. After the Tiger Woods phenomenon, children are now starting as young as age five. While it can be an expensive sport, youth golf programs on municipal courses offer low-cost programs to get young people started.

Equipment: Golf clubs, golf shoes, golf course

Learn more: http://www.usga.org

GYMNASTICS

Acrobatic and tumbling events take place on floor mats and on various pieces of equipment. Men and women both compete in the sport.

Equipment: Gymnastics clothing, floor mats, gymnastic equipment

Learn more: http://www.usa-gymnastics.org

ICE HOCKEY

Considered by most a Canadian game, this sport is played on ice with a puck and stick by both men and women. Competition can require very early or late hours for rink practice time.

Equipment: Helmet, mouth-piece, extensive protective gear, gloves, hockey stick (back up stick), hockey pants, skates, hockey rink

Learn more: http://www.fitness.gov/ice_hockey.html

LACROSSE

Among Native Americans there were many versions of what we now call lacrosse. Players in some tribes used two sticks, one in each hand. Lacrosse, played by both women and men, is a college, professional, and international sport.

Equipment: Lacrosse helmet, protective gear, stick, clear goggles, mesh head, shoes

Learn more: http://www.uslacrosse.org

ROWING

Rowing has its roots in transportation and exploration. It is now primarily a high school, college and Olympic sport for men and women.

Equipment: Single scull, two-man, four-man or eight-man boat, oars, rowing shoes, still waterway / lake or river.

Learn more: http://www.usrowing.org

SKIING

The sport of competitive skiing is only about a century old, but as a transportation method, it dates back over 4,000 years to Scandinavia where Vikings worshipped Ull and Skade, the god and goddess of skiing.

Equipment: Downhill or Alpine competition requires a ski hill and race course. Cross country skiing requires a course on semi-flat terrain similar to a cross country running course. Downhill and cross country skiing both require appropriate attire, skis, ski boots and ski poles.

Learn more:
http://www2.ncaa.org/sports/winter/skiing

Soccer

There is no date of origin for this worldwide sport which involves one ball, kicked only by feet, two teams and two goals. Men and women play this sport from the age of 5 to adulthood.

Equipment: Cleats, protective gear, soccer ball, soccer field

Learn more: http://usyouthsoccer.org

Softball

This game was invented in the early 20th century as an off-shoot of baseball and was intended for indoor play. Softball is a junior high, high school, college and professional sport played primarily by women with a strong following by men in adult recreational leagues.

Equipment: Softball bat, ball, glove, cleats, and softball field

Learn more: http://www.sport-smart.com/links.htm

Squash

Squash is an indoor racket sport played on a court by two opponents. This sport is played by men and women. Courts can be hard to come by but can be found in some YMCA's and Sports Clubs.

Equipment: Squash racket, ball, squash court, shoes

Learn more: http://www.guide-to-squash.org

SWIMMING

Swimming became a competitive sport in England in 1844. Swimming is a junior high, high school, college, professional, and international sport for women and men.

Equipment: Swimsuit, swimming pool

Learn more: http://www.swimmingcoach.org

SYNCHRONIZED SWIMMING

Invented in the early 20th century by Canadian and Australian swimmers, this is a women-only sport combining swimming, Dance and gymnastics. Introduced as an Olympic sport in 1952, competition takes place at the Summer Olympics and World Championships.

Equipment: Swimsuit, swimming pool

Learn more: http://www.usasynchro.org

TEAM HANDBALL

Handball is the newest game within the sport games' category, but its development and origin go back in history, having been played in German schools in the 1890s. Team handball is an international sport.

Equipment: Handball, shoes, court

Learn more:
http://www.funattic.com/team_hand_ball.htm

TENNIS

This is an international sport with competition starting at a young age for both girls and boys and played on a tennis court in singles or doubles matches. Public courts make this an accessible sport for those who want to pursue it. Tennis is a junior high, high school, college, professional, and international sport.

Equipment: Shoes, tennis racket, tennis ball, court

Learn more: http://www.usta.com

TRACK AND FIELD

This sport was played in Olympic Games in ancient Athens as early as the year 776 BC, when Koroibos, a cook from the nearby city of Elis, won the stadium race, a foot race 600 feet long. Track and field involves many different events, some using equipment and some requiring just a pair of running shoes. This is a junior high, high school, college, professional, and international sport.

Equipment: Track spikes, discus, shot put, javelin, pole-vault, hurdles, track, stop watch

Learn more: http://www.usatf.org

VOLLEYBALL

The popularity of this sport was spread by U.S. troops and the YMCA. Volleyball is a high school, college, professional, and international sport.

Equipment: Shoes, knee pads, volleyball, court

Learn more: http://www.usavolleyball.org

WATER POLO

Water polo is a fast and rigorous team sport requiring excellent swimming skills. It is played in high school and college and is also an international sport.

Equipment: Water polo ball, swimsuit, eye goggles, pool

Learn more: http://www.usawaterpolo.com

WRESTLING

Wrestling is a junior high school, high school, college, and international sport.

Equipment: Wrestling shoes, knee pads, head gear

Learn more:
http://uswoawrestlingofficials.com/uswoa_home.htm

sports opportunities. Be realistic about time, budget and scheduling constraints. Consider cross country – all the athlete needs is a pair of running shoes. On the other end of the spectrum, an equestrian requires extensive equipment and access to a horse and riding ring.

Consider the level of participation required, the length of time an athlete can play a sport and accessibility. You can go out and play a round of golf alone or run by yourself. You only need two players for tennis or four for volleyball, but a good game of hockey requires a group and ice time. Also, consider where you live. What's accessible? An ice rink in a small Texas town, for example, may be tough to find. How about longevity? 50-and 60-year olds can still make a great living on the PGA Senior's golf tour, but 30-somethings are wrapping up their careers in football and baseball. There are plenty of adult leagues for softball, basketball, hockey and volleyball, but tackle football may not be an option in later years.

If your child really loves a sport but isn't destined for serious competition, there are plenty of opportunities in training, coaching, management, sales and marketing for professional sports teams.

Are you a family that wants to play together? Consider taking up golf, tennis, skiing, badminton, rowing, running or swimming; something you can all do together. While your children are young, put some thought into the sports you are going to invest in.

Katie Johnson, Student Athlete, College Division I – Volleyball

I started playing volleyball for the first time in 7th grade. I thought I did horribly at tryouts, but I made the team. I wasn't the tallest girl, nor was I even very good, but my parents encouraged me to keep at it. By 8th grade I was a little taller, and I decided to keep playing volleyball. My freshman year, I was playing basketball, which I loved, and playing volleyball, which my heart wasn't into. My volleyball coach recommended that I play club volleyball. She saw potential in me, and my parents went along even though I think they were skeptical. Playing club made all the difference for me. I learned to love the sport and I learned how to improve my performance.

I'm from a very small town where opportunities are limited. In a way that limited my outlook, but my coach pushed me onto bigger things and my parents believed that I could do it. I was determined every step of the way to live up to the potential they saw in me. By junior year I had a really full plate, playing different sports and keeping my grades up. My coaches recommended that I play in a bigger club, so I would get recognized by some colleges, and my parents agreed to drive me an hour and a half each way to practice, three days a week. They were incredible through it all. I played some big tournaments around the country and was recognized by some big schools. I chose to play for Michigan State in Division I competition. I don't know if I would have pursued volleyball because it didn't come easily to me. However, with the help of my coaches and my parents, I was able to improve through learning skills and strategy and learning about my own abilities. In the end, it really paid off.

MAKING THE GRADE

Another key factor in helping your children to become successful athletes is making sure they make the grade in the classroom. Even though children learn a great deal through sports, they have to be just as dedicated to their academics. Becoming a great athlete requires a combination of dedication, discipline, repetition and training; all of the same things that should be applied to schoolwork. Fortunately for parents, most public and private school systems require adequate grades in order to compete on sports teams. While some academic cheating still goes on, the intention is to keep students academically fit. Many student-athletes, regardless of preparation on and off the playing field, do not qualify for college because of poor grades. College scholarships are almost out of the question without better than average grades. Right from the start you should deliver the message that athletic ability must go hand-in-hand with academic achievement.

When I graduated from high school, I knew several great local athletes who held records in track and football and were Division I caliber. Colleges across the nation were recruiting them. But there was one problem: their grades weren't good enough. Their classroom performances didn't match what they had done on the track or the football field.

It's a fact: your student-athlete must perform well in class, have a decent grade-point average, and score high enough on admission tests to be eligible for a scholarship. Let your children know that their athletic ability means very little without a good education. Even those athletes who slip through the cracks and make it to the pros without a good education have limited options when their sports careers are over. Being a successful athlete requires personal and financial management skills along with the social skills that come from a solid education. A good education is essential long after an athletic career is over.

Fred Rush, Father of Charles Rush, Offensive Guard, Penn State Division I Football

We raised Charles to put learning first. Sports are important but just a means to an end, getting a quality education. Too many kids put their whole life into athletics, and this doesn't make sense. Charles has always been involved in his church and his community and is an outstanding football player; who was recruited by 40 different Division I colleges from Boston to Miami and UCLA to Oregon. However, his choice wasn't based on the quality of the athletic program – it was based on the graduation rate for football players. We saw colleges that ranged from a 21% graduation rate and up. Charles chose Penn State which is at 86%. Coach Joe Paterno graduates his players. Penn State also has a very good business program, and it's accessible so my wife and I could get to the games.

You have to face the fact that even if you get into the NFL, football will not be a lifetime career. There are about 1 million high school football players, 44,000 go on to play college football, only about 320 get to the NFL each year, and the average career of an NFL player is about 27 months. Please teach your children that football is not a lifetime career. Your child will play football only *'on the way'* to graduation.

**Look at a day when you are supremely satisfied at the end.
It's not a day when you lounge around doing nothing;
it's when you've had everything to do, and you've done it.**
~ Lord Acton

Olympic Contender, Raffi Karapetian

Tommy Dance, Michigan State Spartans

CHAPTER TWO

PLAYING

Champions keep playing until they get it right.
~ Billie Jean King

LEARNING TO PLAY

We don't *compete* sports or *fight* sports, we *play* sports. Play is creative and unscripted. Even in a sport like football where precise plays are practiced, the player still doesn't know how the defense is going to react. Play is unpredictable. A great player enjoys the spontaneous nature of sports and welcomes the outcome, win or lose.

So, what makes a great player? I think it requires a basic enthusiasm and willingness to engage in the game. No one wants to play with an opponent who isn't trying. A great player is prepared and really knows his sport. He, or she, knows the rules and plays by them. Rules are the only way to measure fair competition. A great player cooperates with his teammates and opponents and is someone who loses and wins gracefully.

The Webster Dictionary's definition of play is "to partake in recreation", and recreation is defined as "any play that is used to relax or refresh the body or mind." Remember that the next time you see an angry parent on the sidelines berating a child or coach. We teach our children to "play to win" but "play" must be the operative word.

Ellie Place, Student-Athlete, Golf

My friend and I went to a driving range to hit some golf balls. After hitting a bucket of balls, we noticed a boy next to us who was amazing. He was about our age, and he was hitting about 200 yards. We were blown away. Then we heard, "*What do you think you're doing? You're doing horribly. Look at your stance; it's outrageous*". It was his dad yelling at him. We just stood there with our mouths wide open in shock just thinking how insane the man was. We went back to hitting balls and having a good time. My mom came over and talked to us about what we could do to improve our swings. We followed her instructions and went back to hitting. Then again we heard, "*What are you doing! Come on, try harder.*" The son looked very mad at his father. My friend and I agreed that we were extremely grateful that we don't have parents like that.

I've heard too many stories and seen too many instances of parents berating their child when the child is supposed to be having fun. A child's spirit can be destroyed by undue pressure and criticism. If you make practice a miserable experience for a child, do you think he is going to want to play and compete? We have to celebrate our children's spirit and enthusiasm if they are going to maintain a great attitude into their adult years. If you take the fun out of play, you will damage more than competitive spirit. You can damage your children's attitude towards success. If winning isn't fun, then why should they bother trying? Encourage your children's willingness to play, and, above all, help them maintain a positive outlook when playing sports. Nothing replaces a good attitude and a joy of playing.

My sons went to school with a boy who had amazing natural athletic ability, but he had such a bad attitude that it destroyed his opportunities in sports. They called him 'Flashlight'. My son Timmy played Little League Football with Flashlight. Timmy gave him the name because he was able to turn his talent on and off like a switch. At age 10, Flashlight was an instant standout. He was bigger, faster and more explosive than the other players. We all enjoyed watching him play. The only problem was that he was a hot head with a horrible attitude, and he listened to no one.

Timmy played with him again in high school, and his attitude hadn't changed. No one could reach him, not the coaches or players. He did what he wanted, when he wanted. The coaches continued to play him just because he was such an outstanding talent, and, as expected, he earned a Division I college scholarship.

His luck ran out in college when he met up with a team of guys who were all hard workers and had positive competitive attitudes. He learned first hand the old axiom that 'hard work beats natural talent when natural talent doesn't work hard'. Flashlight's attitude brought him down, and he was kicked off the team. He learned too late that in the adult world you can't survive on talent alone.

Flashlight's Coach: Anonymous

Many teams have their own Flashlight. Although their talent can be a great benefit to the team, their poor attitude can have an exponentially worse effect on it. I personally coached Flashlight. His talents were indeed remarkable. He possessed athletic ability that surely could have gotten him into the N.F.L, but he walked around with a chip on his shoulder that no one ever understood. Flashlight had a very difficult time communicating his feelings, so his actions were never understood by those around him. As his coach, I felt it was my duty to save him from himself. I felt that I tried everything with the young man to get him to understand the importance of his actions and attitude. I always felt that I needed to help the young man, even after he stopped playing football for me.

As a rule, empathy is a good characteristic for a coach to possess. But in this case, letting Flashlight pull himself out of some of the holes he created may have been better for him. Ultimately, loving and caring about someone too much can be a bigger mistake than practicing "tough love". You see this more often in parents than you do in coaches, but both parties fall into this trap.

There are no easy answers when it comes to troubled youth. It is a tragedy when joy is drained from a child at an early age. And it happens too often. I don't think Flashlight really enjoyed playing the game.

The ability to enjoy play, on any level, tends to keep attitudes in check. Play is about involving yourself in an activity and taking the focus off your own ego. Play is an essential part of our lives. It starts before we can speak. While their children are still in cribs and sandboxes, parents teach them to share their toys and play well with others. From the first game we play with our children, we must also teach them to have fun and follow the rules; cheating is unacceptable. This is the simple foundation on which star athletes build a career. Another lesson in playing is accepting the conditions that we are faced with. There is never going to be a level playing field, perfect weather, or a perfect referee.

Playing the Hand You are Dealt

Norman Vincent Peale, in *The Power of Positive Thinking* tells a story told to him by President Dwight D. Eisenhower. When President Eisenhower was a young boy, he was playing cards with his mother and suddenly threw down his cards in disgust refusing to play his poor hand. His mother gave him a tongue lashing. Mrs. Eisenhower told him that he must always play the cards dealt to him, just as he must deal with all of life's situations as they are put before him. Eisenhower told Peale that it was one of the most important lessons he ever learned.

Young athletes must learn to play and compete according to the rules, deal with the teammates, the coaches and the weather—whatever the circumstances *as they are presented*, without complaint and without bending the rules. How many athletes have we seen who make excuses for bad performances, or verbally attack coaches, umpires and even teammates, to deflect attention from their own actions? That is not the mark of a star athlete.

PLAY FOR HEALTH

Playing is something we do for our minds and our bodies. Teach your children to enjoy playing sports at a young age and they will be more likely to maintain regular exercise in their adult years. Dr. Steve Daniels of the American Heart Association says that the childhood obesity epidemic in our country is a function of both eating habits and the sedentary lifestyles that our children lead. Children are spending their time inside playing video games and watching television rather than engaging in physical activity.

The American Heart Association is promoting thirty to sixty minutes of physical activity a day to combat this trend. Former President Clinton and Arkansas Governor Mike Huckabee have joined forces with the American Heart Association, through the Clinton Foundation, to fight childhood obesity. An important part of their message is the recommendation to UNPLUG! The Clinton Foundation recommends turning off the TV and getting your children out to play, walk or bike. They cite a scary statistic that in 1969, 80% of young people played sports every day; that number is now down to 20%. By age 17, the average child has spent more time watching TV than attending school.

Whether or not children are involved in organized sports, just get them to exercise regularly. A growing number of younger Americans are developing heart disease and having heart attacks. Years ago we would relate heart disease and heart attack to older Americans, but not anymore. Lead by example.

Being a former athlete, I exercised because of my involvement in sports, and it carried on into my adult life. I set an example for my sons, as I hope they will set an example for their children. I haven't always demonstrated the best eating habits, but that changed after my mother died from heart-related problems. I remember that day only too well. My son Tommy came to me with tears in his eyes and said to me, "Dad, you are all we have left, our grandmother has passed and so has our mother. I don't know what we would do if we lost you."

At that moment, I promised my son that I would do everything in my power to take good care of myself so that I'll be around longer - if it is in God's will. Now I do everything I can to control my destiny. I get regular physicals; I have a daily exercise routine, and I control what I put in my mouth. I play for health, and I encourage my sons to do the same.

Taking Play to the Next Step

Once a child is old enough to participate in a competitive sport, the introduction should be fun. What child doesn't want to participate in a fun group activity? Both of my boys started out playing youth hockey at the age of five. They played games on the ice. They had contests. During their days off from practice, we went to the ice rink and played tag and other games that we made up. I always made sure that they were having fun and that they wanted to be there. I think that it is a secret of parents who raise true athletic stars: let your children play and have fun so they really want to come back the next day. A true athletic star has to love the sport, and that first love kicks in at the very beginning. In all parts of life, you have to enjoy what you are doing to be a success.

Athlete - Christine Smith, Field Hockey, Mercyhurst College

I started playing field hockey in 6th grade in New Jersey. I loved playing the sport – I just took to it immediately. In 8th grade I had a coach who encouraged me to join a Futures program for elite athletes, and by sophomore year I was thinking about college scholarships. By junior year I knew I had to play at a level where I would get noticed. My coach encouraged me to go to the national field hockey tournament where I would be seen by college coaches. I did get noticed and received some offers. I chose Mercyhurst College because it was the right fit for me. It's hard playing a sport and keeping up academically, but I really love playing field hockey and that helps. I like the sport so much that I may go on to work for The Future's program as a coach.

When you encourage fun and free play, it helps build self-confidence to try new things and make an extra effort. It allows your child to have fun and improve his skills in the process. Remember that repetition in any sport will build strength, skills and coordination. Repetition and practice do not undermine play; they reinforce play.

If you let your children enjoy their sport, they will play better and will stick with it. They will get respect from their coaches, teammates and opponents if they are a good player. I have taught my sons that winning against someone who isn't playing at their best is an empty win. The real joy in competition is when you are up against the best possible opponent, and, win or lose, you are both playing at your peak. If your student-athletes really enjoy the competition, they will be a much more gracious winner or loser because they will focus on the game and not on the outcome.

TEACHING FAIR PLAY - TIPS FOR PARENTS

From the first time you play a game with your children, you will be teaching them *how* to play. Take a long hard look at your own attitudes regarding competitive sports. Do you believe that winning is all that matters? Or do you sincerely believe in fair play?

"You don't win silver. You lose gold." That was the sour message of a sneaker advertisement aired during the Atlanta Olympics. This kind of message conveys a " winning is everything" philosophy. An increasing number of parents and coaches embrace this way of thinking, making it harder than ever for adults to teach children that it's not whether you win or lose, but how you play the game.

It's not surprising that the rise in outrageous behavior in professional sports has paralleled an increase in poor sportsmanship in youth sports. Trash-talking, violence and disrespect have no place in youth sports. Though we caution our children not to idolize professional athletes who behave badly, there is no way around the fact that young people are influenced by the behavior of the pros.

How can you instill in your child the importance of good sportsmanship and fight the "win at all cost philosophy"? Both parents and coaches can start by focusing on the positive:

- **Be Your Child's Role Model.** Offer praise and encouraging words for all athletes, including your child's opponents. Never openly berate, tease, or demean any athlete, coach or referee while attending a sporting event.

- **Be a Good Sport's Fan.** Be mindful of your behavior when watching sports. What messages are you sending your child during the Olympic games if you honor only athletes from the United States, while rooting against athletes from all other countries? Let your child see you enjoy sports. Embody the philosophy that you don't always need to win or be the best to enjoy playing sports.

- **Do You Have A Hidden Agenda?** Be honest with yourself about why you want your children to play organized sports. What do you want them to gain from the experience? Are your intentions based on providing them with fun, social activities that develop a better sense of self-worth, skills and sportsmanship? Or do you harbor dreams of them turning their topspin forehand into a collegiate scholarship or riches and fame? Check your own ulterior motives.

- **You Set the Rules.** It's ultimately your responsibility to teach your children good sportsmanship, both as a participant and as a spectator. If you observe your children engaged in poor sportsmanship, talk with them about it, whether their coach corrects them or not. If a coach is ignoring, allowing or encouraging poor sportsmanship, you need to make your objections known to the coach *in a private discussion.*

- **Watching and Learning.** Whether you're watching the Olympics on TV or attending a high-school sporting event, you can always find "teachable moments" regarding sportsmanship. Ask your children their opinion of players who showboat and taunt their opponents or about the costs to the team for a technical foul. Talk about the appropriate behavior of opposing players towards one another after a game.

TEACH GOOD SPORTSMANSHIP FROM THE SIDELINES

Teach good sportsmanship by example. Show respect for your children, the game, the coach, officials and opponents by staying on the sidelines and out of the game. Don't argue with referees, don't coach your children from the sidelines, and don't argue with other parents of children on your team or the opposing team. Children will learn how to play – by example.

Kathleen Avitt, The National Alliance of Youth Sports (NAYS)

Most parents show proper respect at their children's games, but the few that don't, spoil it for the rest. You can do something about it by supporting the code of behavior provided by the team's administrators. The school board or sports program board of directors should have a code of behavior for your child's sports program. The effectiveness of the code of behavior depends on how it is communicated to the parents. Simple rules and strict consequences should be communicated, agreed to and executed. Do your child a favor and support the rules. Experts agree that the simpler the code of behavior, the better. It should address everyone involved, from the team members to the fans.

Kathleen Avitt says that her organization sees a dramatic difference in the behavior of parents after they go through the NAYS - PAYS (Parents Association for Youth Sports) educational program regarding parental rights and responsibilities in youth sports. Their parents' code of ethics is taught to parents and is then communicated and enforced during competition. Kathleen says that they don't see a lot of violations, but, when they do, there is a review committee in place to review the violation, and they take action. The program teaches parents that sports are not all about winning. The goal of the National Alliance for Youth Sports is to make sports and activities safe and positive by providing programs and services that add value to youth sports. There are many not-for-profit organizations like NAYS and The Center for Sports Parenting that you can contact for information regarding sports parenting programs.

Dan Doyle, Executive Director of the Institute for International Sport at URI, and co-founder of The Center for Sports Parenting warns against excessive codes of behavior. "You don't want to create an aura of being a moral IRS agent. Keep it simple and focus on civility and sportsmanship."

If your child's sports program has a code of behavior that is too complicated, poorly communicated or is not enforced, offer to help improve the situation. A simple code of behavior can be four or five points that include the conduct of all participants. It can be read by an official before each game and posted in locker rooms and near the stands. Officials can be reminded at each game to enforce the code.

It's also important to understand why parents have become overly aggressive when it comes to their children's sports. Dan Doyle sees parents becoming excessively involved with their children's sports because they think they can help their child attain an athletic scholarship for college. He points out that financial aid is so readily available and athletic scholarships are so hard to come by that putting all of one's effort into athletic achievement just doesn't make sense. I agree with Dan's assessment. The possibility of an athletic scholarship is slim. It is something to work towards but not count on. Parents need to calm down. Help your child balance academic and athletic achievement. Let your child enjoy his time on the playing field.

On the subject of excessive parental involvement, Dan says "At the Center for Sports Parenting we promote balance. I suggest pursuing Aristotle's rule of the golden mean - seeking balance between deficiency and excess. Be involved but not too involved. "

I've enjoyed watching my two sons learn this tough lesson on their own, that winning is not everything. There may be times in their athletic development when winning takes over as the number one priority. Just as I did with my sons, I encourage you to work through these periods and continue to teach good sportsmanship and a love of the game; be there for them when they need you.

Timmy Dance, Gannon University Football Player

I remember when winning wasn't everything; just to be out on the field and be able to play was a reward. It was when we played a game and no one kept score. It was when I received a trophy after a wrestling match and didn't even come out on top. Sorry to say, at some point in my athletic career, winning became everything, the only thing that mattered. I guess it all started in my own back yard playing sandlot football. It was always my friends and I, versus another group of kids from around the block. We played almost every day. We played in the rain, snow and mud. If we lost to the opposing team, bad attitudes would show, and we would even start fighting with each other. When a sandlot team in our neighborhood would win, they would talk trash everywhere they went especially at elementary school. The talk would continue until the teams met again. For that reason alone, the thought of losing became agonizing.

From elementary school all through junior high school, my thought process remained the same, "I simply can't lose; I have to win." I had to win for the girls, the fans, my family and my friends. I had to be on top or all hell would break lose. It took a State Championship football game my junior year of high school to change my whole mentality about winning and losing. We were ranked in the top 10 in the country as were our opponents. This was said to be the high school game of the century. We battled for 59 straight minutes. The crowd was on its feet, and televisions around the country were tuned in to the game. We had the ball in the fourth quarter with 1 minute left to go with the score 13-7 - us. On fourth down we decided to punt the football out of our own end zone, and it was blocked for a touchdown with under 2 minutes left in regulation. We ended up losing the game 13-14. Then, as was our tradition, we prayed and gave God thanks and praise for the opportunity to play the game we love in front of thousands of fans. After that game, I realized that some athletes would have killed to be in my shoes that night. I was fortunate just to have played in that atmosphere.

On the long bus ride home the little boy inside of me who had played sandlot football in his backyard told me that I would be back for vengeance. He told me that I would be back because I had worked so hard, and this loss would make me and my teammates work harder. That alone picked me up and put the biggest smile on my face. I had a talk with all of the players who would be returning for the next season. I told them about the talk that I had had with myself. I promised them that if we gave thanks to God, believed in ourselves and worked even harder, we would be back.

The following year we went back to the state championship game and played the same team from the prior year and we won. It was incredible and a true Cinderella story.

I've won a lot of games in my life, but none of them taught me as much about character, perseverance or, most importantly, my belief in God. That loss we faced my junior year turned my life around and made me a man.

The Right to Play

Sports should be the great equalizer in this country, but discrimination and economic barriers have plagued sports in America since the beginning. Help your children learn about the athletes who have paved the way for equality in sports. These great athletes didn't let barriers stop them; they just wanted to play the game.

Jackie Robinson, Major League Baseball Player

In 1941, Jackie Robinson became the first athlete in the history of UCLA to letter in four sports (baseball, football, basketball and track) in the same year. After 3 years in the army, he had a short stint in the Negro Leagues, and then he broke baseball's segregation and became a symbol of hope for millions of Americans when he signed with the Brooklyn Dodgers. The Dodgers won six pennants in Robinson's 10 seasons, and he was named National League MVP in 1949, leading the league in hitting (.342) and steals (37), while driving in 124 runs.

Jim Thorpe Greatest Athlete of the 20th Century

Born in 1887, Native American Jim Thorpe was called the greatest athlete of the 20th century, excelling at every sport he tried. He played football for the Carlisle Indian School and later for the New York Giants. He won the decathlon and pentathlon events at the 1912 Olympics and played major-league baseball from 1913 to 1919. Jim Thorpe was selected by the nation's press in 1950 as the most outstanding athlete of the 20th century and was also declared "America's greatest football player of the half-century."

William Taten Tilden II - Professional Tennis Player

Bill Tilden won his first major title at Wimbledon in 1920 at the age of 27. He was also the first American to win at Wimbledon. He won 10 majors, 3 at Wimbledon and 7 in the US. When his homosexuality was publicized, he was shunned from the tennis world and banned from the most prestigious tennis courts. Despite these troubles, in 1949 he was voted the most outstanding athlete of the first half of the twentieth century by the National Sports Writers Association, with ten times the number of votes as the nearest runner-up.

Jesse Owens - Olympic Gold Medalist Track and Field

Jesse Owens was an African-American sprinter and one of the greatest track-and-field athletes of all time. As a member of the U.S. track team in the 1936 Olympic Games held in Berlin, Owens won four gold medals and set new records in the 200-m dash, 400-m relay and running broad jump. Because Owens was black, Adolf Hitler refused to acknowledge him. Nevertheless, he went on to many future victories and played an active role in youth programs until his death in 1980.

TITLE IX – LET THE WOMEN PLAY

In 1950, Kathryn Massar of Corning, NY, tucked her hair under a baseball cap and tried out for Little League. She wasn't out to prove a point or pick a fight; she just wanted to play baseball.

She made the team and was allowed to play. However, in 1951 a new rule was introduced into Little League regulations: "Girls are not eligible under any conditions." Teams who allowed girls to play were threatened with having their charters revoked.

It wasn't until 1972 when Little Leaguer Maria Pepe was asked to leave her team that the media and the National Organization of Women took notice. The case went before the New Jersey Civil Rights Division where examiner Sylvia Pressler declared as part of her ruling: "There is no reason why that part of Americana should be withheld from girls." In 1974, over 30,000 girls signed up for the newly formed Little League Softball. Since then, over 5 million girls have participated in Little League.

In 1971 President Richard Nixon signed Title IX into law, and women were granted equal opportunities in high school and college sports. The law also increased funding for high school and college athletics. Young female athletes should never take Title IX for granted. Please encourage your daughters to take full advantage of the opportunities and to remember the women athletes and law-makers who have made it possible. There is a lot of money that goes unused each year for women's athletic scholarships. If you have a daughter who is interested in sports, look into the scholarship opportunities in her sport while she is still young. In the past decade, female athletes have proven that being athletic is not antithetical to femininity. There are great female athlete role models who have gone on to raise families and have exciting careers but who have benefited immeasurably from sports. Get your daughters into the game!

Babe Didrikson Zaharias, Professional Golfer, Co-Founder LPGA

Born Mildred Didrikson, Babe earned her nickname when friends compared her to the great Babe Ruth during a sand-lot baseball game. Her athletic career started in 1930 at the Employers Casualty Company of Dallas where she instigated the company's semi-professional women's basketball team, the Golden Cyclones. Between 1930 and 1932, she led the team to two finals and a national championship and was voted All-American each season. She then went on to represent the company in track and field and qualified for 1932 Olympics where she broke world records in three events, winning gold medals for the javelin and hurdles.

In 1932, after setting her sights on professional golf, she entered and won the Texas Women's Amateur Championship and soon met George Zaharias, a well-known professional wrestler and sports promoter whom she married on December 23, 1938. Babe went on to win seventeen consecutive tournaments, including the British Women's Amateur Championship, the first American to do so. Didrikson helped found the Ladies Professional Golf Association to provide the handful of professional women golfers with a tournament circuit.

In April 1953, Didrikson underwent surgery for cancer, and despite predictions that she would never play championship golf again, she was in tournament competition fourteen weeks later. The Golf Writers of America voted her the Ben Hogan Trophy as comeback player of the year. In 1954 she won five tournaments, including the United States Women's Open. She died on September 27, 1956, at the age of 45.

Do you remember why you play, or has it been too long? Is it because you've worked so hard to get where you are, or because you love to be part of a team? Is it because you don't want to let anyone down, or yourself? Somewhere behind the athlete you've become, the hours of practice, the coaches who pushed you, the teammates who believed in you and the fans who cheered for you, is the little boy who picked up a ball, who fell in love with the game, and never looked back.... Play for him.
~ Unknown

Chapter Three

Believing

It's lack of faith that makes people afraid of meeting challenges, and I believed in myself.
~ Muhammad Ali

I Believe in You

Four little words, "I believe in you," can change a child's life. If you believe in your children they will learn to believe in themselves. Strong beliefs give children the courage to do their best and make good decisions. It will drive their inner voice that tells them what to do when no one is looking. Belief determines how student-athletes feel about their own abilities, the competition, their team and coach. Be a parent or coach who lifts children up to their potential by helping them build a strong belief system.

**Cliff Crosby, NFL Cornerback, Kansas City Chiefs –
Super Bowl Winner**

My first great coach was John Dahlstrand. He was probably the most important coach in my life because he helped me build confidence. As a kid, basketball was my first choice in sports. I didn't really think I was big enough for football. During football season, I would worry about getting hurt and not being able to play basketball. Coach Dahlstrand told me that I could be good at football, and he just kept telling me that he believed that I could do it. It's easy to let yourself down, but when someone else believes in you, it's hard to let him down.

Another great coach in my life was Ron Vanderlinden, who went on to Penn State. He really told us the truth all the time – good or bad. Some of the other players didn't like it, but it was good for me. At one point, I had a bad eye injury and had to have surgery, so I was out for a good part of the season. I didn't expect to play right away, but Coach Vanderlinden put me in as soon as I was cleared. I was overwhelmed. I didn't think I could do it, but he told me he believed in me. I went in and played well because I didn't want to let him down.

If you teach your children that winning is everything, they will believe that only winning is important and that they must do whatever is necessary to win. Athletes who fear losing learn to blame the weather, the playing conditions, the officials' calls or their teammates to deflect attention away from their own performance. They may learn to cheat by breaking rules or taking drugs to help their performance. What do you want your child to believe in – the game or the win?

The "win at any cost" mentality is corrupting our children. When athletes cheat, it's because they don't believe in themselves, the coach, or the team. I was taught at an early age to walk by faith and not by sight. Student-athletes have to have faith in themselves and their preparation in order to compete at their highest level.

Faith is the substance of things hoped for, the evidence
of things not seen.
~ Hebrews 1:1

I've thought about how I helped my sons believe in themselves. It came instinctively; it was always there. I told them over and over that I believed in them, and I showed them by asking them to always try their best. Throughout their athletic careers, there have been coaches, teachers, family members and teammates who reinforced the message. It is so important to know the people who are influencing your child. Get to know your children's' coaches and teachers. Talk with them in private about your standards and your rules. When my son's high school track coach, David Woodard, told me, "I don't coach cheaters," I knew that we were in sync. That simple statement summed up his belief system for me.

Saying to a five-year-old "I don't raise cheaters," gives a clear and simple message with a monumental life lesson behind it. Plain and simple, cheaters don't deserve the time and attention of anyone, much less sports professionals. Think of the cheating that goes on in sports, academics, business and politics. Cheating destroys lives, teams, companies and economies. Cheating is a constant temptation that will present itself throughout your child's life. As parents and coaches, we can give a child the power to choose right over wrong. One of the best places to teach your child to follow rules is on the playing field. Competition will test your child. Young athletes can't help but see easy opportunities to bend the rules. Calling 'ins' as 'outs', faking injury, inflicting injury, falsely crying foul: it's all there for the taking. Tell your child that you believe that cheating is wrong.

The first time you catch your child cheating, use it as an opportunity to teach him that he is accountable for his actions. There is a price to pay, and that price will get much bigger as your children get older. Talk to them about respecting the game. The only way to measure the outcome of a competition is by following the rules of a game. If athletes cheat, the competition is invalid. Everyone loses. You can put it on a grand scale and talk about steroid use in professional baseball. The fans, the players and the owners have all lost because of cheating and greed. Record books are invalid, fans are disappointed, and players now compete under a cloud of suspicion and drug testing.

Telling your children that you believe in them means that you believe they can succeed without cheating, without drugs and without bullying. Praise your children's accomplishments, and praise their honesty in admitting mistakes. Help them find role models who have failed, tried again and then succeeded – without cheating.

Timmy Dance – Gannon University – College Football Player

My dad always told me that sports would teach me about life, especially when it comes to learning about how to deal with success and, more importantly, disappointments.

Disappointment is like a man climbing up a tall hill, almost reaching the top and falling down. When he falls to the bottom, he might consider himself a failure, but he has only failed if he quits and refuses to try to reach the top again. That man could fall one hundred times, but succeed on his 101st attempt. There are many famous people today, not just athletes, who fell down that hill but refused to quit and are now successful.

- Michael Jordan was cut from his high school basketball team at the beginning of his sophomore year.

- A teacher told Martin Luther King, Jr. that he would never be able to speak with enough emotion to inspire people to take action.

- Young Thomas Edison's teacher told him he was too stupid to learn anything.

- Beethoven's music teacher once said to him that as a composer he was "hopeless."

If Michael Jordan had quit his team, at what level of play would the game be today? No one ever said it was easy to get back on that hill and keep climbing. When I fall, I ask Jesus Christ to pick me back up and give me the strength to climb again. When athletes or teams fall, they have to find that special something that lifts them back up.

Take the first step in faith. You don't have to see the whole staircase, just take the first step.
~ Dr. Martin Luther King Jr.

Keeping the Faith

When your child experiences tough times, his faith will help him get through it. In the dark of the night we have to believe that the sun is going to shine again, and so it will be in your child's athletic career. I have shared most of the good with you. I want to share some of the more challenging times with my sons.

As everyone knows, some student-athletes have a tendency to become arrogant and overly confident about their skills. They should never think they are invincible. As parents of talented athletes, we have to keep our children humble and not allow them to get swelled heads. But I know this is easier said than done.

At one point my oldest son, Timmy, having experienced a lot of success, turned arrogant. He learned the hard way that he was not above reproach. Timmy had just come off of the biggest games of his college career, piling up record yardage and completions. This was a young man who had enjoyed great success all through high school and college; you can imagine how he felt. It was hard enough just to support the weight from his big head; "humility" was not part of his vocabulary.

After a big out of town game, Timmy and his friends went to a bar to celebrate. Timmy got into a fight and seriously injured the man who had provoked him. After an arrest, mug shots and a night in jail, my son was charged with a serious crime and faced a felony charge with a mandatory minimum prison sentence of two years. Timmy tells his own story later in the book, but from my point of view it was the worst possible nightmare. I thank God that we had our faith to see us through.

I cried that day out of fear for my son, as well as out of deep disappointment, a pain I know most parents will feel. Even though Timmy did not initiate that confrontation, he was responsible for his actions. We have to help our kids understand when they are young that there are consequences for their actions. Your children must believe in themselves but never to a point where they take advantage of others. A belief in what is right and what is wrong comes first.

In Timmy's case, the charge was later reduced to a misdemeanor, and he was allowed to keep his scholarship and continue participating in athletics. But the experience humbled him. He discovered the hard way that it is safer and wiser to be a man with two feet planted firmly on the ground — except when he runs for a winning touchdown.

The Gordons

Beverly and John Gordon raised three outstanding female athletes, Tiffany, Chelsea and Sheena. These girls not only excelled in their sports, they all exhibited courage in the face of serious challenges. After interviewing their parents, it was clear to me that this was all because of how they were raised and the beliefs handed down to them.

Sheena Gordon received a full track scholarship to UCLA. After two years she transferred to The University of North Carolina where she also received a full scholarship. In 2002, she was honored with an invitation to compete in the Olympic trials, a dream come true. She competed well, successfully completing two rounds of her high jump when she was denied from continuing on to the next round. Sheena made sure she fully understood the denial, calmly went to the rule book herself and found a ruling that she used to protest the decision. She was denied again, and again she appealed based on the rules. On a third appeal, she was allowed to continue in the trials.

Even though she didn't make the Olympic team, competing in the trials was a treasured experience for her. She tells other athletes that they have to keep their faith through the ups and downs and play by the rules. Sheena believed all along that God had a plan for her and she always stayed faithful and positive no matter what.

Beverly Gordon on daughter Sheena:

I was with Sheena on the day she was eliminated from the Olympic Trials. After several rounds in the high jump, she was eliminated. I didn't know that the ruling was questionable, but Sheena did. I didn't know how to protest, but she found the rules that addressed her situation and very respectfully explained her position to a group of officials. There were judges with 20 or more years of experience packed into a little trailer listening intently to her. Everyone agreed with her position except the official who had initially ruled against her. It was clear to me that the official did not want to admit that she was wrong. Without being rude or disrespectful, Sheena handled the situation with great confidence. It took hours, yet she stuck with it until she had won her case and was able to go on in the trials. What struck me was that she didn't need me there, and for that I couldn't have been prouder. My husband has always taught our girls that if they have a valid point, they must stand up for themselves, even against authority figures. We have been realistic about the girls going off on their own, and we knew that they needed to learn to speak up for themselves, especially in competitive sports environments. We didn't shelter them. We wanted them to experience the real world as soon as possible.

John Gordon on his daughter Chelsea:

Our oldest daughter Tiffany was a great basketball player but had to stop because of chronic back pain. Her younger sister Chelsea, who had always been a real "girly girl", surprised us all and followed in Tiffany's footsteps. She developed into a talented basketball player, basically on her own. She had to work harder than the other girls because of her size, but she stuck with it. She eventually became a starter on an elite team, but she was sidelined because of a serious injury. She worked her way back to competition but was then injured again in a serious car accident. Her second comeback was even tougher because she was afraid that she would re-injure herself. She lost a lot of confidence in the process. The coach wasn't playing her but that was ok; we taught our kids never to blame the coach. Chelsea knew that she had to earn the right to play and she did. She came back even stronger and went on to a full basketball scholarship at the University of Illinois.

We have taught our daughters that their talents are a gift from God and that they must be thankful. It is a blessing for a child to be able to achieve her dreams. I have always had high expectations for them because I believed they were capable of them, and we have taught them to have high expectations for themselves. If you don't expect more, you don't get more.

BE THEIR ROLE MODEL

Child psychologists talk a lot about giving children roots and wings. You need to ground your child with the proper belief system and also give him the confidence to leave the nest and fly on his own. Sports can help with this daunting responsibility. What we teach our children about right and wrong on the playing field applies to every other aspect of their lives. Competitive sports can ground children with a sense of self-responsibility and can fuel them with the self-confidence to succeed on their own.

Belief must be demonstrated to take hold. Words aren't enough. The first time a parent watches a child play a potentially dangerous sport and doesn't run in and stop the game, he is demonstrating belief in his child. You demonstrate your belief when an official makes a call that you don't agree with, and you remain silent on the sidelines. You demonstrate your belief in your children when you give them room to succeed on their own. Sometimes, the hardest thing to do as a parent is to do nothing at all. Have faith in your children.

Walk the talk. It doesn't matter what you say, it's what you do that counts. They are going to pay attention to your actions. Let your children know that you believe everything you are telling them. Stop bending the rules, on the golf course, running traffic lights or cheating on your taxes.

Andre Agassi, World Champion Tennis Player, was asked if he would encourage his children if they want to play tennis. His answer was that he would encourage them only after they took ownership of their goals. He said that he didn't truly take ownership of his own destiny until he fell back to a world ranking of 140. That was his wake up call, and he worked hard to come back to be a champion again in his 30's. Agassi now runs a school in Las Vegas for disadvantaged youth. He is an athlete of integrity and character. He is a wonderful role model for his children because he is living his belief in hard work and education.

Attitudes

If you think that all parents are teaching their children to do the right thing, you are wrong. There are very scary statistics revealed in the following sportsmanship survey from the Josephson Institute of Ethics. I sincerely hope that when you pick this book up again in five years, you will look back on this survey information as reflecting the darkest period of youth sports in our country. Let's start mentoring a new generation raised to practice good sportsmanship.

New Survey Shows High School Sports Filled With Cheating, Improper Gamesmanship And Confusion About Sportsmanship

High school sports do teach positive values and build character, but in many cases young athletes -- especially males -- learn to cheat, engage in improper gamesmanship and indulge in excessive violence. In the wake of the 2004 Olympic Games, with nearly two dozen disqualifications for illegal drug use and several controversies centering on sportsmanship, a new survey of over 4,200 high school athletes provides a chilling picture of a confused generation floating in moral relativism and self-serving rationalizations.

The study conducted by the CHARACTER COUNTS! Coalition (a project of the nonprofit Josephson Institute of Ethics) is believed to be the most comprehensive measure of the attitudes and behaviors of high school athletes.

According to the Institute's president, Michael Josephson, "The values of millions of youngsters are directly and dramatically influenced by the values conveyed in high school sports. This survey reveals that coaches and parents simply aren't doing enough to assure that the experience is a positive one. Too many youngsters are confused about the meaning of fair play and sportsmanship, and they have no concept of honorable competition. As a result, they engage in illegal conduct and employ doubtful gamesmanship techniques to gain a competitive advantage. It appears that today's playing fields are the breeding grounds for the next generation of corporate pirates and political scoundrels." Among the key findings:

- **Girls Are More Sportsmanlike Than Boys.** The attitudes of boys and girls who participate in sports vary dramatically. Overall, males are far more likely to exhibit cynical attitudes and engage in illegal or unsporting conduct.

- **Coaches Don't Always Set a Good Example.** While nearly 90% of high school athletes report that most of their coaches set a good example of ethics and sportsmanship (Q2), it's not clear they know what a good example is. Large portions of these same athletes endorse questionable actions of coaches including: 1) **arguing with an official intending to intimidate or influence future calls** (51% of males, 30% females) (Q43); 2) **instructing players how to illegally hold and push opponents without getting caught** (45% of males, 22% females) (Q32); 3) **using a stolen playbook** of another team (42% of males, 24% females) (Q48); 4) saying nothing when an official **declares the wrong score in favor of the coach's team** (a mathematical rather than a judgment error) (40% of males, 21% females) (Q47); 5) **instructing a player to fake an injury** to get a needed extra time out (39% of males, 22% females) (Q31); 6) ordering a pitcher to **throw at an opposing hitter in retaliation** after a key player was hit by a pitch (30% of males, 8% females) (Q29); 7) **swearing at an official to get thrown out of a game** in order to get the team worked up (38% of males, 12% females) (Q49); and 8) using **profanity and insults to motivate players** (37% of males, 15% females) (Q50).

- **Many High School Athletes Break Rules and Engage in Unsporting Conduct.** Judging by the conduct and attitudes of young athletes, it appears that many coaches place winning above the concept of honorable competition and sportsmanship by teaching or condoning illegal or unsporting conduct. Thus, high percentages think it is proper to: 1) **deliberately inflict pain in football to intimidate** an opponent (58% of males, 24% females) (Q30); 2) **trash talk a defender after every score** (47% of males, 19% females) (Q34); 3) **soak a football field** to slow down an opponent (27% of males, 12% females) (Q40); 4) **build up a foul line in baseball to keep bunts fair** (28% of males, 21% females) (Q35); 5) **throw at a batter who homered last time up** (30% of males, 16% females) (Q33); and 6) **illegally alter a hockey stick** (25% of males, 14% females)(Q37).

· **Cynical Attitudes About Success**. Nearly half of the male athletes reveal cynical attitudes about the prevalence, necessity and legitimacy of cheating in the real world. Thus, high percentages agree with the following statements: 1) "in sports, **people who break the rules are more likely to succeed**" (30% of males, 15% females) (Q10); 2) "in the real world, **successful people do what they have to do to win even if others consider it cheating**" (56% of males, 45% females) (Q5); 3) "**a person has to lie or cheat sometimes in order to succeed**" (43% of males, 27% females) (Q6); 4) "**it isn't cheating if everyone is doing it**" (19% of males, 9% females) (Q11); and 5) "**if you're not cheating, you're not trying hard enough**" (12% of males, 5% females) (Q12).

· **Winning More Important Than Sportsmanship**. 1) More than one in three males (37%) -- versus only 15% of the females -- agree that "when all is said and done, **it's more important to win than be considered a good sport**" (Q14). 2) While 94% of the females agree that "**playing the game fairly and honorably is more important than winning**," 20% of the males disagree (Q4). 3) While 87% of females believe that a high school **coach "should** be more concerned with character building and teaching positive life skills than winning," more than one in four males (27%) disagree (Q8). 4) 31% of males and 25% females believe their **coach is more concerned with winning than in building character** and life skills (Q7).

- **Correcting Referee Errors.** 1) 22% of athletes say it's improper if, on the winning point of the game, a volleyball **player says nothing after the referee misses the touch** before the ball goes out (48% think this is acceptable, 30% were unsure) (Q42). 2) 24% believe it's improper if a referee calls a ball out in tennis, but the **player definitely saw it hit the line, says nothing and takes the point** (46% say this is acceptable, 30% were unsure.) (Q44).

- **Fooling the Referee** 1) About half the athletes (52%) think it is improper in basketball if **one player is fouled and a different player, the team's best free-throw shooter, goes to the line** undetected by the referee (21% found it acceptable, and 27% were unsure) (Q39). 2) 49% say it's improper if a player in soccer, during a penalty kick, hoping the referee will not call it, **deliberately violates the rules by moving forward three steps past the line before kicking the ball** (22% found it acceptable and 30% were unsure) (Q41) . 3) 41% say it's improper for a soccer player to deliberately fake a foul hoping the best player on the other team will be red carded and removed from the game. 31% found it acceptable; 28% were unsure (Q45).

- **Putting Sports Above All.** Only half of all athletes (52%) think it is improper to hold an academically successful student back a grade so he will be older and bigger when he plays high school football; 25% say they are unsure (Q53).

- **Performance Enhancing Drugs.** 1) 12% of the males and 3% of females **used performance enhancing drugs** in the past year (Q27). 2) 78% of the males and 91% of females agree that "no athlete should use performance enhancing drugs because it is **unhealthy**" (Q15). 3) 78% of males and 87% of females agree that "no athlete should use performance enhancing drugs because it is **cheating**" (Q16).

- **Playing More Important Than Winning.** As a counterpoint to the winning obsession, 72% of both males and females say they would rather play on a team with a losing record than sit on the bench for a winning team (Q18), and more than one-fourth of the males (28%) -- as opposed to only 13% of the females -- say that winning is essential for them to enjoy the sports experience (Q19).

- **Cheating and Theft.** In the past year: 1) 68% of both males and females admitted to **cheating on a test** in school (Q20), 2) 26% of the males and 19% females said they **stole something from a store** (Q21), and 3) 43% of the males and 31% females said they **cheated or bent the rules to win** (Q26).

- **Hazing and Bullying.** 1) 31% of males and 17% of females report that **degrading hazing or initiation rituals** are common at their school (Q17). 2) 69% of the males and 50% of the females admit that they bullied, teased or taunted someone in the past year (Q22). 3) 55% of the males and 29% of the females said they used racial slurs or insults (Q23).

Reprinted from Josephson Institute of Ethics Sportsmanship Survey 2004 with permission of the Josephson Institute of Ethics.©2004 www.josephsoninstitute.org

INTEGRITY

Integrity is the ability to choose right from wrong, even under peer pressure. Honesty, sincerity, completeness - these are the things that make up integrity. When your children are asked if they want to do drugs, to help a teammate cheat, or to haze a new student, it will be their integrity that keeps them from giving into the temptations. If your children learn to believe in themselves and in right and wrong, they will build the integrity to see them through the toughest challenges.

Too many so called superstars have lied in the face of steroid use accusations, claimed not to have known what they were taking, or blamed it on their trainers or coaches. These superstars clearly lack integrity. Teach your children that if they make a mistake, big or small, they must own up to it, correct it and learn from it – not shy away or lie about it. That's integrity.

STICKING WITH IT

Spiritual and mental strength for athletic achievement starts with a positive attitude. Parents and coaches bear the responsibility of instilling self-confidence in young athletes. We constantly have to remind them that they can 'do it'. Eventually your child will learn to believe in his own abilities.

Sometimes we are called on to discern the fine line between encouragement and force. When my youngest son Tommy started playing ice hockey, he did not show the same interest as his older brother Timmy. I came to see that this was not due to a lack of interest, but was because he didn't like getting up early for practice on weekends. He would rather have slept late and then played video games. I would not let my sons quit in the middle of a season. I let them know that when the new season arrived, they wouldn't have to play if they didn't want to. In life there are times when things get tough, but we must continue to push forward regardless of the obstacles. I wasn't going to force him to participate in something in which he had no interest, but I wanted him to finish what he had started.

Coach Kirk Ferentz - Iowa Hawkeyes
NCAA Division I Football
Advice for Youth Coaches

I advise youth coaches up to 10th grade not to focus too much on the scoreboard. Everybody keeps score, but it shouldn't mean everything. Even at the college level, we don't talk too much about winning; we talk about doing things the right way and improving. We talk about how you treat your teammates and we focus very heavily on improving. We teach our players to be smart about their decisions.

At younger levels – teach fundamentals – emphasize good and honest effort and trying to improve skills and be a team player. For youth coaches, I recommend that you send your players home happy, so that they want to come back and play the next day. Build them up and make it a great experience.

Children must enjoy their sport or playing will do them no good. They will come to resent the time and effort. It's one thing to ask your child to try this or that in order to find a fit, but if your child reveals a lack of interest in a particular sport, honor his decision.

Encouragement makes a fault easy to correct and a
challenge easy to take on.
~ Dale Carnegie

TEENAGE YEARS

As your student-athlete grows and develops mentally and physically, he or she will enter the true competitive years in athletics, years during which both you and your child will be faced with many ups and downs. Now the athlete faces competition for a place on a team and starting positions. He must contend with the frustration of not always being out on the field during games. This is when an athlete learns about loss. It is when he will need you most and will draw on what you taught them as a child.

Nothing is worse than seeing your son or daughter in tears. The teenage years can be the most emotional, so this is the time when your children will really depend on your consolation and support. Sports and academics parallel the highs and lows of life in general. Athletics serve as preparation for life, so it is doubly important to help them grow and learn during this difficult period. Adult life is going to be full of joys and disappointments, and sports can teach your child how to handle disappointments. When I related events on the field to real-life experiences, my boys understood and felt better. I always framed the lesson in a way that they could understand, so they would come back fighting harder the next time. Don't be afraid to put in your two cents – you are the parent!

**Confidence comes not from always being right
but from not fearing to be wrong.**
~ Peter McIntyre

Tommy Dance - Michigan State Spartans – NCAA Division I Football Player

A man can be as great as he wants to be. If you believe in yourself and have the courage, the determination, the dedication and competitive drive and if you are willing to sacrifice the little things in life and pay the price for the things that are worthwhile, it can be done.

"Once a man has made a commitment to a way of life, he puts the greatest strength in the world behind him. It's something we call heart." (Unknown)

To become the best, you must make sacrifices. To accomplish your goals you must put all other things aside and focus on what you believe in. You must realize that all hard work pays off in the end. You must then be ready for adversity in the life you have chosen for yourself. The way you handle yourself will determine your future and destiny.

You must be able to handle everyday life and the way society is. This is the process of coming to realization with oneself. It could help to develop a personal relationship with God, who is our Lord and Savior. All things are possible through Jesus Christ. You must realize that God will never give you something that you are unable to handle. You must go beyond the expectations of others to be the best at what you do. You have to be willing to do the extra things in life to get to where you want to be.

"You all have powers you never dreamed of. You can do things you never thought you could do. There are no limitations in what you can do except the limitations in your own mind as to what you cannot do. Don't think you cannot. Think you can." (Unknown)

Remember that you can do anything in life as long as you apply yourself and do the things necessary to obtain that goal. The only person stopping you from doing what you want to do in life is you. You must first take on a positive attitude and use all of the negatives as strength and motivation. There are no limitations if you're willing to make the sacrifices that come with success.

FINDING POSITIVE ROLE MODELS

Children of any age can use role models to help them learn to believe in their own abilities. You can point to older brothers and sisters, relatives, friends and pro athletes. Find great role models for your students in their chosen sports. Talk to your children about how these athletes came to believe in themselves and how they used their fame for the benefit of other people.

> **Anytime you have an opportunity**
> **to make things better and you don't,**
> **then you are wasting your time on this earth.**
> *~ Roberto Clemente*

Roberto Clemente

Known the world over as "The Great One," many believe Roberto Clemente was the greatest right fielder ever to play the game of baseball. Throughout his career, he set numerous other records and led the Pittsburgh Pirates to two World Championships. He recorded his 3,000th hit on September 30, 1972, and also has the distinction of being the first Latino to be inducted into the Baseball Hall of Fame. But that was not his greatest achievement. As writer John Snook points out, "This was a man who could have lived a luxurious life away from the troubles of society and the poverty he faced as a child, yet, he was not like that. He gave up his life trying to help other people in need." In 1972 he died in a plane crash off the coast of Puerto Rico on his way to take medical, food and clothing supplies to earthquake stricken Nicaragua.

A strong belief system will empower your student-athlete to do something important with his life. Tell your child that if he gives his best then he can never be a loser. You've got to believe to succeed.

If you can reach out, you can hold on.
If you can imagine, you can achieve.
If you can begin, you can continue.
Search within, and you'll be rewarded with the taking.

If you can get involved, you can make it happen.
If you can give, you will be rewarded with the taking.
If you climb, you can climb even higher.
Envision it; your success is in the making.
If you trust the winner within you, you will win.
If you can keep the courage, you will go so far.
If you follow your ambitions, your course will guide
you towards a ladder that you can climb to your stars.

If you don't put limits on yourself,
you can always keep striving.
You might amaze yourself with
what you discover you can do.
If you want to reach out for happiness,
don't forget these words:
You can go as far as your dreams can take you.
~ Collin McCarty

Chapter Four

Training and Nutrition

The road to success runs uphill.
~ Willie Davis

Physical training and good nutrition should be a priority in everyone's life, especially children's. Start your children off with good habits at a young age. There has been an alarming increase in the cases of childhood obesity in the U.S., but parents can help fight the trend if they just help their children get a minimal amount of exercise everyday and make healthier food choices. I don't care if your children ever play organized sports; just get them off the couch. Replace the cookie with the carrot, and get your children moving.

Training

Training is something children do without realizing it. It may sound like overkill to start five-year-olds on a training program, but in reality, they started training before they could talk. Training is just repetitive instruction or an application of motion that develops a skill, a muscle group or a belief system. Your children start training the first time they put a spoon to their mouths or lift themselves from the floor to take their first steps. Remind your children that they have been training for something their whole lives. They started from nothing, and they progressed until they reached their goals, whether it was feeding themselves, walking or learning to talk.

The key to early training is motivation. Toddlers are motivated by the promise of independence and the desire to communicate. They'll keep trying until they can walk and talk. In later years, motivation dies down because young people become satisfied with the status quo. It is the same with athletes. Somewhere along the line, student-athletes choose to either reach for greatness or settle for what they have. How student-athletes choose their path is based on two things: they must have the desire to compete at a higher level and they must be physically prepared. The will to win means nothing if the athletes haven't received the proper skills training, or aren't in the right physical shape to compete.

Look beyond sports when you are talking to your children about the need to train for extraordinary performance. Things that seem impossible to one person are possible to another because of training. Ask a firefighter how he runs into burning buildings when others are running out. Ask a pilot how he learned to fly a jumbo jet. Ask Lance Armstrong how he won the Tour De France after battling cancer. It's all about training.

Proper training is a balance of mental and physical practice. Skill development comes from physical repetition, and mental toughness comes from developing a belief system. A child can train to hone skills but still be an impossible brat on the playing field. I believe that so-called superstars who exhibit horrible behavior did not receive the right balance of training. Focusing on skills alone doesn't work.

Training Starts with Learning Good Sportsmanship

Good sportsmanship is sometimes best taught by pointing out bad sportsmanship. Athletes and parents who scream and yell and throw tantrums are the best advertisements for 'what not to do'. It's embarrassing, and nobody wants to play with a bad sport whether it's a weekend golfer who throws his clubs or a little leaguer who throws tantrums. To really get your point across, turn on the TV. There have been some unforgettable athletes who have served up great examples of bad sportsmanship. John McEnroe is remembered as the bad boy of tennis, gaining fame for his bad language and degradation of officials on the tennis court. Tonya Harding's attack on fellow Olympic skater Nancy Kerrigan overshadowed all figure skating competition for a season. Will NBA pro Ron Artest be remembered for his jump shot or for charging a fan in the stands? Winning and athletic achievements do not make up for unsportsmanlike behavior.

So what is the solution to the problem of bad behavior? Train for good behavior. When you first introduce your children to a sport, base their training on the best role models and the best examples of how the sport should be played. Talk to your children about the athlete's physical strength, skills and sportsmanlike behavior. These are all by-products of the training that the athletes have received during their careers. Remember that there are many more good sports than bad sports out there. Unfortunately, it's the bad ones who get all the publicity.

I'm trying to draw a line in the sand here. Let's train student-athletes to compete at the highest level but also behave with dignity and believe in their sport, their teams and their fans.

MENTAL FOCUS

When your children start to take training a bit more seriously, ask them to imagine themselves at the top of their sports. What would it be like to be soccer star Mia Hamm or Michael Jordan or Tiger Woods? Professional sports are showcased in competition, not training. Talk to your children about the years of training behind the big moments. Talk about what it would take to become a respected, successful professional athlete. Challenge them to imagine the hard work and commitment that it takes to get to the top, and discuss what would happen if they didn't make it. Would the hard work still be worth it? You can't force-feed a fire in the belly, but you can lay out all the information your children need to make some important decisions about their futures. You can motivate, participate and support your student-athletes missions to achieve their goals. Goal setting is a great life skill for your children to learn at an early age. If they plan to excel in their sports, they must set goals for training and competing.

Goal setting involves mental focus and commitment. You can teach mental focus at an early age. You can show your children that they can have fun and still be focused on what they are doing. Teaching young children how to concentrate can start with something as simple as sitting and reading a book for 10 minutes or attending a concert where they will have to sit quietly and listen. Athletic stars must work on developing concentration throughout their lives. The ability to be in the moment, concentrating on one point, goal or skill, is a true mark of an athletic star. The famous baseball player Charles Ray Knight once said, "Concentration is the ability to think about absolutely nothing when it is absolutely necessary." Learning to be in the moment is another life lesson from sports that will serve your children through their lives. Mental focus and self-control are essential for success in academics, relationships, work and that inevitable, endless PTA meeting that they will have to sit through someday.

SELF-CONTROL

Teaching a child self-control will pay off in all areas of competition. Children need to know how to handle cheap shots and cheating on the part of teammates and opponents and bad calls from referees. Talk about situations where they will be challenged and discuss how they should handle themselves. Teach the rewards of self-control and the consequences of reacting inappropriately. Just one violent reaction can get a child kicked off a team or out of school. Young athletes have to learn that competition isn't always fair, a great life lesson for children. Practicing patience and self-control should be an important part of your training program.

INTENTION

Teach your children about having intention when they train. Their intentions can be towards making an extra effort, focusing on teamwork or trying a new technique. Intention in training translates to purpose in competition. Children who compete with purpose are far more likely to win than those whose hearts aren't in the competition. It can also take the focus off the scoreboard and onto the game. I see some athletes who would be just as happy to beat a team 100 to 1 as to win 100 to 99, just as long as they win. The win becomes all that matters, not the purpose of competition.

I taught my sons that a true athletic star enjoys winning the most when the competition is the toughest. Being a star isn't about 'beating' another team or another competitor. Being a star athlete is about loving the game, sportsmanship and being able to play at the highest level against the best athletes. Share the excitement of a close game played by two great teams or any type of championship where competitors revel in playing at the top of their game. Help your children imagine what it would be like to be athletic stars who have trained with the best coaches, who have played with the best team, and who are able to compete against the best athletes.

SKILLS TRAINING

Goal setting is another life skill that comes from athletics. When you start training, even with young children, try to set short and long-term goals. Short-term goals can revolve around commitment and skills development. Help your children commit to a certain amount of reps or to an amount of time they will practice each day. Try to make it fun. Long-term goals should be achievement-based. They are the personal reward for sticking to the short-term goals. If your child walks a mile with you every other day, a long-term endurance goal might be a 10-mile hike. Batting practice for a half-hour a day may lead to a long-term goal of a first trip to a batting cage.

No matter what the sport, you can isolate specific skills and use practice drills to develop those skills. Plenty of individual athletic skills cross many different sports. Sprinting is necessary in baseball, track and field, tennis and football. You can run short sprints with your children anywhere and make a game out if it with their friends. Any sport with a ball and bat, racket or club requires great hand–eye coordination. Try an egg toss to practice manual dexterity – with raw eggs. Get creative. Soccer, cross country and swimming require endurance. Go the distance with your children, walking, swimming or running. Talk to your children's coaches about his or her recommendations. Practicing drills at home will help children focus on different aspects of a sport and help them to decide what position or what type of competition best suits them.

Use the journal in the back of this book for short-term and long-term planning. Stay flexible with short-term goals which may change, but try to stick to milestone goals and long-term planning. From my experience, I don't think that you should let your child switch sports without finishing out the season or reaching a long-term goal.

TIMMY AND TOMMY

When my sons started running track, I continued to supplement the coaching they received at school. We worked on their starts in the starting blocks. Timmy, who was undefeated in the 100 meter race in his junior and senior years, wasn't great at the start. We knew that with his overall talent, if he could improve on that one area of weakness, he could really excel in the sport. If we could improve his start, then he could start going after some records. My younger son Tommy was not only the 100-meter champion, but he was two time state champion in the 110 high hurdles and a national qualifier. He trained well beyond the scheduled practices with the team. Several times a week after practice, when the rest of the team was at home or hanging out with friends, Tommy and I went to a gym for strength training. There were many days Tommy didn't feel like doing it, but I gently reminded him what champions are made of. In addition to weight training, Tommy needed to work on his hurdling skills on the track. It was the extra training that helped both of my sons to excel in sports. It was their commitment and my patience that helped get them to the next level.

Let your younger child know that a seventeen-year-old doesn't suddenly wake up one morning and decide to go after a college athletic scholarship. Long-term planning is essential. You don't have to be a "stage mother" pushing your child to distraction. Quiet, consistent support and guidance can help your children reach their potential.

A Conversation to Have with Your Children

Help your children imagine their sports heroes at their own age. Where did they start, how hard did they work and how did their parents or coaches help them? Ask your children to imagine how the sports figure went from having little or no ability to where they are today. Remind your children that it all happened through training, dedication and determination.

Around the age of 10 to 12, your children can start developing their own training programs, setting their own bigger goals. Help them stick with their goals. Be realistic about what it takes to stick with a training program and practice schedule. Time demands, physical demands and intrusion on academics all play a part in the big picture. Are you willing to get up Saturdays at 6 am to get rink time? Will you be able to drive an hour every day to the closest pool or afford to send your child to gymnastics camp for the summer? Ask yourself and your children: "What is it going to take to commit to a training program? How am I going to stick with it? Is the reward worth the effort?"

Raffi Karapetian - College Swimmer, Olympic Contender

I was taking swim lessons at a summer club when I was 11 years old and a swimming instructor recognized that I had some talent. In what seemed no time, I was swimming meets, I got onto a winter team, and, by age 14, I was swimming at a state level winning several events and breaking some state records. By age 15 I was receiving recruiting letters from college coaches.

My practice times were crazy, often at 5:30 in the morning, a half hour from home. But I stuck with it because I loved the sport and I understood the importance of training at an early age. I love swimming because it's you against the clock, it's about your personal performance and your training efforts, and there are no variables. In tennis you are playing someone else who may be an easy or tough opponent, and in other sports, there's the weather and all kinds of external factors.

In high school I was invited to the Olympic training center with 25 other top swimmers. It took me to a whole new level in my attitude toward training and competing. The next year I accepted a full scholarship to a Division I college. I had a pick of schools but I made my choice based on the reputation of the coach. He had trained a number of Olympic swimmers.

I hit a wall in my first year of college. I wasn't swimming well and I knew something was wrong with the way I was training. I was really upset and my coach was surprised at my poor performance, too. At one meet I swam slower than in my early years in high school. At one particular meet, I had a really bad day and I called my Dad from my hotel. He must have heard how depressed I was because the next day he flew out to California to be with me. My parents' support really got me through some bad times.

Things didn't get much better the next year, and my coaches knew that I wasn't swimming as fast as I could. I wasn't enjoying practice for the first time in my life. There was definitely a cloud over my head. With the help of one of the assistant coaches, I made the decision to transfer to another college. This time I talked to a lot of coaches and I concentrated on their training techniques. I was definitely in a position to make a better decision based on the coach and what I needed. I was a sprinter and I needed the right kind of training program to get back to my best.

I transferred to a Division II college with a great coach whom I had known previously. The training program and the school were a great fit and before long I was training correctly and winning again.

Training has always been great for me because I feel so much better after practice. If I was having a bad day, practice helped me. Now that I'm in medical school, swimming helps me relax, and the discipline of training when I was younger definitely helps me in school.

BALANCE

I believe in balanced training programs. Common sense dictates that overuse of a specific muscle group is not smart. A child shouldn't train twelve months a year in the same sport. It causes burnout and injury. Cross-training is necessary for the mind and the body.

"Tommy John" surgery, for injuries resulting from excessive movement repetitions, is now rampant among child baseball players. Some sports programs are taking steps to limit the amount of training and practice allowed in certain age groups.

THERE ARE NO SHORT CUTS

A few pro athletes have bragged that steroids have made training unnecessary for them. Let's look at this: By taking steroids, they are compromising their health, their mental stability and their credibility. So I guess they are correct - steroids have made training unnecessary for them – and steroids have made them unnecessary athletes. Talk to your kids about steroids and all illegal performance enhancement drugs. They don't make sense. Only through training, can an athlete become a true athletic star.

Mike Goodwin, Certified Personal Trainer, Owner American Fitness, Cathedral Prep High School Football Coach, Erie Pennsylvania, Strength Training for Student Athletes

Weight training for athletics is more popular in today's sports then ever before. Training for almost all sports includes weight lifting. Athletes in non-contact sports are also now beginning to include weight training to improve their performance.

Weight training can give an athlete an edge by building explosive strength and muscle endurance. Examples of explosive strength would be a lineman's block in football, or a boxer's punch, or a sprinter's start and muscle endurance is needed for sports like cross-country running or long distance swimming.

Training, will make an athlete stronger, quicker, and also improve his or her jumping ability. Professional athletes in today's sports are bigger and stronger then ever before, so athletes are starting to weight train at a younger age.

At any age, it is important to have a program, preferably designed by a professional. Training programs will be different depending on factors such as age, experience, and individual sports. All programs should be individualized for the athlete using them. There isn't one standard weight training program for every athlete. Athletes starting a weightlifting program should be under the supervision of a personal trainer, coach or qualified person.

Younger athletes between the ages of 12-14 years old should start weight training on machines that provide a full range of motion. Machines are safer for a younger athlete. Free weights can be introduced to a program when the trainer feels that the athlete can control the weights through a full range of motion. Younger athletes can also benefit from exercises such as push-ups, sit-ups and pull-ups. Young athletes should stay away from heavy weight lifting because it could lead to injury.

All athletes who use lifting in their training, especially younger athletes should be trained on how to stretch before and after every workout. Maintaining flexibility while weight training is essential for optimal athletic performance. Weight training for any length of time without maintaining flexibility will lead to strains, pulls and muscle tears.

When the athlete is introduced to free weights, i.e. barbells and dumbbells, he or she should always push or pull the weight through a full range of motion with full control of the weight.

The weights should not increase until the trainer feels the athlete is strong enough to control the weight. Once the athlete develops muscle control he or she can be introduced to more advanced free weight movements such as squats and *dead lifts* These lifts must be supervised to ensure proper form. Athletes 12-14 years old should lift no more then 3 days a week. A good training routine for the young athletes is to break up the 3 days into a push, leg and pull work out. The push day would be concentrating on chest, shoulders and triceps. The pull day would target the back, traps and biceps.

Most sports programs will use the same basic lifting movements in the routines but may vary the number of sets and reps they perform. Almost all sport programs will include some type of weight training. The athlete who starts weight training at a younger age has a big advantage over those who don't.

NUTRITION – THE BASICS

Teach your children about good nutrition and hydration. Healthy children are more inclined to be healthy adults. Even if your children never step foot on a playing field, you owe it to them to teach them about healthy eating habits. As the parent of young children, you have almost complete control over what they eat, and you can teach them good habits by example.

The USDA Food Pyramid is always changing recommendations for a healthy diet, but some basics remain constant such as providing a balanced diet of vegetables, whole grains and proteins and limiting fat and sugar. What is important here is that your children understand the basic components of the foods they are eating, how the food helps or hurts their performances, and how it affects their health. Extreme diets and unsafe supplements are not the answer for good health or optimum performance.

Be a good role model for your children's eating habits. If you are eating things that you tell them not to, what do you think they are going to eat? I often thought that because I wasn't a smoker and I didn't drink, I must be in pretty good condition. Not true. After I turned forty, I had a complete physical and on the surface everything looked great. My doctor was amazed. I had the body fat of a teenager and I looked and felt great. He ran some blood tests and when the results came back several days later, my cholesterol level was far too high. Realizing that high cholesterol levels can lead to heart disease or heart attack, I was frightened. My doctor scheduled another appointment with me to come in and discuss what we could do about the high cholesterol levels. I had horrible eating habits and they had caught up to me. I did a lot of research online and learned how to read food labels and avoid foods that weren't good for me. I am proud to say that changing my eating habits has brought my cholesterol down to safe levels without having to use prescription drugs. Once I educated myself about healthy eating habits, I passed what I had learned on to my sons who have also changed their eating habits.

Here's an idea: no matter what the age of your children, make a pact with them that you'll start eating smart if they do. It's really about common sense. Knowing what certain foods provide in the way of energy, vitamins, minerals and calories will come with time. Just pay attention to what you eat and talk to your child about what they are putting into their mouths. Learn how different foods affect the body and athletic performance. A candy bar right before a long baseball game is not going to do children any good. It will only provide a short burst of energy that could leave them with low blood sugar long before the game is over.

Try this; the next time you go to the grocery store, stick to buying fresh fruits and vegetables, whole grain breads, cereals, nuts, beans, low fat protein, cheese and dairy. Avoid processed foods and foods laden with salt, sugar or fat. The "good foods" are found mostly on the outer aisles. Think *fresh* and *unprocessed*.

BASIC COMPONENTS
FLUIDS

Without proper hydration your children could put their health at risk during training sessions and competition. You cannot say it often enough : "drink your water" and "don't get dehydrated". Check to make sure that water is always available to your child during the school day and during practice and that they are encouraged to DRINK IT!

Dehydration causes fatigue, even in the cold. It will decrease performance, impair cardiovascular function and can pose serious health problems. An athlete can become dehydrated after as little as 30 minutes of exercise.

During exercise, working muscles raise the body's temperature. To get rid of the heat, we sweat to cool the body which causes dehydration. The simple antidote is to drink plain old water. You don't need sports drinks, just water.

Things to make your children aware of while they exercise, and it's all about the sweat:

- **Temperature**: The higher the temperature, the more you sweat.

- **Intensity**: The harder you work out, the more you sweat.

- **Body size**: The bigger the athlete, the more you sweat, and males generally sweat more than females.

- **Duration**: The longer the workout, the more you sweat.

- **Fitness**: Well-trained athletes sweat more. And they start sweating at a lower body temperature. Why? The function of sweating is to cool the body. The well-trained athlete cools his or her body more efficiently than a person who is out of shape. You can't rely on thirst as an indicator of dehydration. Get your children into the habit of drinking water before and after exercise. Water also cleans out the system. Drinking eight – 8-ounce glasses of water a day, with or without exercise, is a very healthy habit to get into.

CARBOHYDRATES

There is a fad diet, that hopefully will die soon, that recommends cutting out almost all carbohydrates. That just doesn't make sense for you or your children. Of course there are good and bad carbohydrates. Teach your children about the good carbohydrates in whole grains, dairy, fruits and vegetables.

Carbohydrates power the brain and body. Think of them as fuel for your muscles. Exercising with low levels of carbohydrates leads to fatigue. Carbohydrates are stored as glycogen in the muscles and liver, maintaining blood sugar. A person needs to maintain a consistent level of blood sugar for clear thinking and physical performance. A large amount of refined sugar (carbohydrate) will provide a "sugar high" and then drop you right back down. Low blood sugar creates fatigue. To keep it simple, avoid *simple* carbohydrates (candy, soda, bakery goods, table sugar) and eat complex carbohydrates (whole grains, beans, starchy vegetables, fruits, and dairy products).

Fat

No-fat diets don't make sense for anyone, especially not for athletes. Fats, like carbohydrates, are used as fuel and also help the body absorb certain vitamins. Fats also help carbohydrates continue to 'work' during endurance events. Aim for a low-fat and 'good' fat balance in your diet, no more than 30%, and that should be adjusted based on body weight and level of activity.

There are good and bad fats. Make it simple. Olive, canola and nut oils are good; animal fats and butter should be limited. Stay away from anything 'greasy' and limit fried foods. And stay away from hydrogenated oils, found in cakes, cookies and margarine. Teach your child to read food labels.

Protein & Amino Acids

Protein is necessary for muscle maintenance, but it's the most difficult nutrient to digest. Your body expends a lot of energy just breaking down high-protein foods. Avoid large amounts of protein before training. As with all nutrients, eat protein in moderation. Low-fat meats, chicken, eggs, low-fat dairy, cheese, yogurt, nuts, natural peanut butter and green leafy vegetables are great sources of protein.

Above all, keep it simple, learn as you go and stress that all people feel better, perform better and have a better shot at a long, health life if they eat right.

Injuries and Healing

Another inevitable component of training will be injuries and recovery. Whether they are small or serious, every athlete suffers a setback from time to time. Too many athletes are forced back onto the playing field before they recover completely from an injury. This can lead to a long-term disability. It's just not worth it.

Prevention is the name of the game. If you can prevent an injury, then you won't have to incur the time, expense and pain of recovery. Prevention starts with knowledge. Know how to prevent injuries in your children's chosen sports. It may be learning extra care with equipment, stressing safety precautions or avoiding overuse of certain body parts. Make sure you and your children's coaches have a common understanding about the steps needed to prevent injuries.

Dr. Keith Lustig Orthopedic Surgeon and Sports Dad

Overuse injuries such as tendonitis in the elbow region, whether from youth pitching in baseball or softball or moms and dads golfing, can be very painful and take the joy out of a sport. As always, the best treatment is prevention. In young athletes it is most important that they do not inflame sensitive areas by repeated use. The common sense answer is to limit your repetitions whenever signs of overuse develop. A sensible way of doing this is to adhere to good cross-training principles. Parents, trainers and coaches should all work to develop good workout programs and not just send athletes out to " hit golf balls until your elbows get sore". The surgeries that have been developed for chronic tendonitis are obviously the final attempt to cure and should only be necessary in a few athletes who have failed to improve in spite of significant programs of rehabilitative exercises and time off from exacerbating activities.

My son Josh was playing in the Rambler's final regular season game against the local high school from the Penn State University town of State College, PA. He had been the leading receiver for three years on the nationally-ranked Rambler football team. At a crucial point in the game he ran a deep post route and dove for a ball making a great over-extended catch. As the fans were cheering the noise was slowly dampened as Josh lay flat on the ground, obviously injured. When he struck the ground, he had held onto the ball but had sustained a complete fracture of his clavicle (collar bone). He walked to the bench with his trainer and seemed to only be bruised or winded from the fall. My wife and I then got into a debate about whether I should go down on the field to check on him or not. The debate stopped as his trainer looked up in the stands and waved me down onto the field. As a dad, I was sure there was nothing serious going on; the playoffs would be starting the following weekend and that meant five weeks until the state championship game. As an orthopedic surgeon I knew the first thing I was going to do was feel his solid clavicle and then be relieved that he was only shaken up on the play; after all, he had held onto the ball so there was no way he could have been seriously injured. As I looked him in the eye and told him he would be fine, I lifted his jersey and felt his clavicle. It was obviously fractured in the mid-shaft, not the best place to hope for quick healing, in fact, the most common site for a fracture that sometimes is very difficult to heal and finally requires surgery. Again, being a dad, I assured him that it was indeed fractured but that he would be back before the state championship game. Since Josh was a great competitor, this didn't help much as he broke into tears, knowing that he would now miss several games.

As the next few days evolved, he had several relatives, friends, and school officials telling him that broken bones take six weeks to heal, meaning that he would miss the state championship game if the Ramblers were indeed persistent enough to get to it. At home it was a different story. My wife, older son, and I decided (after significant mother/father/brother debate) that we would leave the final call to our in-house orthopedic surgeon. Luckily, the team doctor was happy to pass this possible controversial decision to me.

For one week, we kept Josh in a sling; well, maybe it was more like three days. I slowly moved his shoulder in three days but the pain was still significant when attempting more than 20% of normal motion. At about one week we had increased his motion to 90%, but he was still in a sling. When I initially told Josh he could possibly be back in four weeks and play in three more games he said, ''Come on dad , don't try to make me feel better.'' Being the macho dad I told him, "I'm really not concerned with how you feel; I'm giving you my honest opinion." After 10 days of slightly diminishing pain he made a significant breakthrough. I remember when I first saw him on that Tuesday, he had a huge smile and said, "Hey, Dad, it really feels good today; it hardly hurts at all." We went out in the front yard and he tried to catch a few short, soft throws. Not too bad but he knew he still had a ways to go.

From that point on things improved everyday. He missed a bye week and two games and that brought us to Thanksgiving which was 3-1/2 weeks post injury. I went to practice with Josh and told Coach Mischler that he would possibly be ready for the Altoona game that was 2 days away. Mischler sounded very excited but somewhat apprehensive about my statement. "Do you mean he could actually be cleared to play; how will we know if he's ready?" I told him. "Misch, if you get in a spot where you really need him, he can do it."

As the Altoona game progressed, it looked like the team of champions needed just one little spark to help them pull out a win. The team was playing solidly, but something was missing. At that point Coach Mischler looked up to me in the stands and asked for the ok, or more specifically for medical clearance for Josh to return to full contact. Following a quick consult with Mary Kay, or I should say a very quick consult, I gave Misch the thumbs up. In the third quarter Josh went in, and, on a fourth down in overtime, caught his second pass of the night to help give the Ramblers the win and the opportunity to play in the state semi final the following week.

Josh is now in his final year on the William and Mary football team. He lettered in his first three years and will start as wide out this fall. Knowing how much the sport means to a son is a blessing for a mother and father, and having been fortunate enough to be an orthopedic surgeon allowed me to see my son through a difficult time and help him recover earlier than he might have otherwise. It led to a great father son experience that we will both remember for a long time. Possibly more important than the memory is how this experience helped our relationship grow. Trust, support and encouragement were all very positive things that came out of this experience.

Another great example of handling a serious injury comes from a young professional baseball player. Zac Cline was a good friend of my son's at Cathedral Prep High School in Erie, Pennsylvania. He was recruited out of college by the Philadelphia Phillies baseball organization as a left handed pitcher. He is one of a small percentage of student-athletes who have gone on to professional sports, and he is a fine example of an athletic star. My admiration for him is not because of his ability to play baseball but because of his winning attitude and his ability to handle an injury that could have been taken as a serious setback by most athletes.

Shortly after graduating from West Virginia University, he was recruited by the Phillies. He wasn't on the team very long before he was faced with the ubiquitous 'Tommy John' surgery and the realization of a long rehabilitation. Through it all, his work ethic and lack of self pity have been admirable. When I asked him how he maintained his positive attitude he told me that it was his up-bringing. His father was his coach up until high school and his dad taught him that talent only takes an athlete so far. Zac learned that discipline and hard work are the difference between a good athlete and a great athlete. Zac modestly told me that he never considered himself the best pitcher or the hardest thrower, but he was a hard worker. He considers hard work the most important character trait that an athlete can possess.

Take your children's training seriously, but keep it light – no pressure, just consistency. Take training beyond skills to good sportsmanship. Teach mental focus and self-control. Your student-athletes will learn personal behavior that will pay off for a lifetime.

Ellie Place, Junior Golfer

CHAPTER FIVE

TEAMWORK

**The way a team plays as a whole determines its success.
You may have the greatest bunch of individual stars in
the world, but if they don't play together,
the club won't be worth a dime.**
~ Babe Ruth

The first time your children assist in a goal, complete a pass or win an individual competition that contributes to a team win, they will know the thrill of teamwork. Learning to be a good team player will serve athletes in all aspects of their adult lives. Knowing how to be a good team player is an essential skill in sports and business, as well as in community and volunteer activities. A good team player is more likely to get a good job, be promoted, be asked to participate in projects and get invited to play in social sports as an adult. Beyond the fun and the competition and the great memories of being on a team, your children will benefit from learning how to rely on others and how to yield to others.

START YOUNG

Learning to play well with others starts early – in sand boxes and play pens. Teamwork starts with sharing, support and sacrifice. From an early age you can teach your children about teamwork in almost everything they do. Teach them to share their toys, and share their thoughts and feelings. Communication is a very important part of teamwork. Show your children that you are willing to share your thoughts and your expectations of them. If someone needs help, lend a hand. If there is something that needs doing at home, show your children that you are willing to do it. Be a role model in teaching your child about teamwork. If you are a team player, your children will learn to be team players.

From the first time your children play a game, you can teach team working skills. Whether it's a board game, a card game or tossing a ball in the backyard, teach cooperation - with everyone in the game. It's as simple as teaching children how to throw the ball back to you instead of over your head, or dealing the cards to you instead of all over the table. Teach in small consistent steps.

Alone we can do so little, together we can do so much.
~ Helen Keller

When your children start playing sports, pay close attention to their behavior towards other teammates. See how well they cooperate and how they deal with the more aggressive players on the team. Wait for a good time to talk, preferably not right after a game. Give your children time to digest what has happened in the game. When you talk about their interactions with teammates, ask them how they felt about the player who hogged the ball or threw a tantrum or sulked on the sideline. Chances are, your children don't like selfish behavior. Reinforce that notion. Let your children know that a 50-year old tennis player who poaches the tennis ball on every occasion is just as aggravating as an 8-year old who always hogs the soccer ball. Let your children know that you want them to be gracious sports – for life. Good sports are usually asked to participate; bad sports aren't.

Pay close attention. Are your children the ones who hog the ball or are benched for most of the game because of bad behavior? Work with your children when they are young, when there is still time to help them learn the importance of teamwork. The following are a few things that I focused on with my sons.

TEAMWORK

Performance - You have to do your best for the sake of the team. If the individual team members all do their best, then the team will do its best.

Cooperation – Do what the coach tells you to do and don't fly solo. A team needs a leader. Follow his or her instructions, and trust his or her judgment.

Support – Help your teammates. Work with them to do what's best for the game. United you stand, divided you fall.

Role Models – Find positive role models for your children in their primary sport and in other sports.

Great Team Players in Sports History - Magic Johnson

One of the best team players who also gained personal fame was basketball legend Magic Johnson. When it came to performance, Earvin "Magic" Johnson was exceptionally skilled and truly enjoyed his sport. When he was a child, he would dribble with one hand all the way to his neighborhood store and dribble back with the other. He developed outstanding personal skills and exhibited unselfish team play. He was an NBA All-Star 12 times in his 13-year career. He was named NBA MVP three times, in 1987, 1989 and 1990. His outstanding team play is illustrated by his leading all-time assists (10,141) and his steals (1,724) record. Johnson was the NBA's all-time leader in assists until the record was broken by Utah's John Stockton in 1995. Johnson dazzled fans with his passing abilities. Lakers swingman Michael Cooper said of him, "There have been times when he has thrown passes and I wasn't sure where he was going. Then one of our guys catches the ball and scores, and I run back up the floor convinced that he must've thrown it through somebody."

It has been said of him that he achieved greatness while maintaining a childlike enthusiasm and a love of the sport. He was just happy to play basketball.

He has also given plenty back to the youth community in many different ways including HIV/AIDS awareness programs. He admitted his HIV diagnosis in an effort to help young people avoid a similar fate.

Some children are going to hog the ball and focus on selfish gain; some are going to pass the ball and focus on team play. If parents and coaches teach great teamwork, the outcome will be rewarding for everyone on the team, not just the superstars.

Elizabeth Place, Mother of Ellie Place, Jr. High Student-athlete

My daughter Ellie, an only child, didn't start playing team sports until fifth grade. She grew up playing golf and tennis so we secretly wondered about her ability to work well on a team. In her first season of softball, she played starting catcher and was awarded *The Sportsmanship Award*. In seventh grade she managed the boy's soccer team and was awarded *The Coaches Award* for teamwork and positive attitude. I don't think her father and I could have been more proud of her. While skills and performance are important, it's the sportsmanship and teamwork that are going to pay off when she is an adult.

Teamwork is complicated and difficult. It's easy for a coach to consistently play the better athletes. It takes time and patience to develop the other athletes, but it's worth it. Some teams can win relying on the performance of one player and ignore the rest of the team. But what if that one player gets hurt? There are practical reasons to teach team play and invest in team development. If you see a coach consistently playing the same athletes and benching the others, it's time to say something - in private. That coach is not promoting teamwork.

Great teamwork among student-athletes sometimes involves group decision making. This is an incredibly difficult skill that most adults have yet to grasp. Children often are faced with tough decisions in team situations, whether or not to cheat or whether or not to haze a new athlete. This is where team leadership comes to play. Make sure that your children are the ones who stand up for what's right and lead their teams away from bad decisions. Character building begins with the first few tough choices that a child has to make.

Tommy Dance

In my memory one specific day stands out as a great exhibition of teamwork. It was day two of my track meet, and we were already predicted to lose. Many of the points that we had anticipated on the first day had been lost on the field events. The fate of our team was dependent upon not only the athletes who still had to compete but also on support from the athletes who had already competed. When I was warming up, I noticed the involvement from every teammate surrounding the track. It was obvious that no one from the team had given up. It didn't matter what anyone outside the team thought because we believed in ourselves. One race at a time, the point gap started to close, and we could see the championship was still within our reach. Going into the last race Coach told us that in order to win the meet, we had to win this race. It was the 4x400 relay, and one of our runners was injured. Coach asked one of my teammates who had never run this event to step up and help the team. It was very close throughout the entire race, but in the end we won by about 50 meters. As a team we accomplished what no one else thought possible.

A SENSE OF COMMUNITY

Playing on a team should teach children to focus on common goals and away from individual personalities. Teamwork should help children learn how to get along with people that they may not necessarily choose as friends. That's the life lesson in teamwork they will take on to school, to work and into their communities. Good team players benefit everyone. Talk to your children about focusing on the common goal of working together and cooperating. Whether that goal is winning a game, a tournament, or a Division title, children should learn at an early age to put their egos and personal feelings aside and do what's best for the team.

Ask yourself, "What characteristics does a good team player possess?" Talk about it with your student-athletes. By Webster's definition, teamwork is 'a joint action by a group of people', the operative word being, joint. It is a rare team where everyone gets along well off the playing field. And that is precisely what makes it an excellent learning experience for children. Becoming a good team player requires putting aside personal differences and joining together to play at peak performance in order to win. Good teamwork is a combination of performance, cooperation and support.

> *Remember team, surrender the me for we.*
> *~ Phil Jackson, Six-time NBA Championship, Head Coach*

MONEY CAN'T BUY TEAMWORK

Seek out coaches who understand the power of teamwork and encourage it. Every coach that I have interviewed for this book agrees that being a team player is at the top of the list of attributes when they are looking at new recruits. John L. Smith, football Coach of the Michigan State Spartans, told me that when he is recruiting, he looks for athletes who are going to be great team players, not the superstars who are only concerned about their personal records.

It's not about money either. You can't pay an athlete to be a great team player. Two particular team efforts that stand out in my mind are the 1980 US Olympic Hockey Team and the 2004 U.S. Olympic Men's Basketball Team. One was a rag-tag long shot that won because of hard work and extraordinary teamwork; the other was a group of some of the highest paid athletes in the world who never jelled as a team. Olympic teams are fascinating to me because they are temporary, and the will to win isn't all about money but national pride. An Olympic team may end up playing in competition together only a handful of times, but it's on a world stage.

1980 US Olympic Hockey Team:

Remembered by some as the greatest team victory of the 20th century, this group of college hockey players took on a seemingly invincible Russian hockey machine and beat them.   "It may just be the single most indelible moment in all of U.S. sports history," said Sports Illustrated of Team USA's improbable gold medal run at the 1980 Winter Olympics.

Herb Brooks, an NCAA coach at University of Minnesota and student of international hockey, was known for his rough personality and his perfectionist attitude towards preparation. Brooks didn't just throw this team together; he spent a year and a half building a team and putting them through a difficult schedule of exhibition play prior to the Olympics. The players included Neal Broten, Dave Christian, Mark Johnson, Ken Morrow and Mike Ramsey, who would go on to impressive NHL careers. There was no chance to outmatch the Russians in skill. Instead the coach worked on speed, conditioning and discipline. Because the team members had been college rivals, one of the greatest challenges was uniting them as a team, which the Coach accomplished at the expense of his own relationships with the individuals.

2004 US Olympic Men's Basketball Team

This team lost to Italy, Puerto Rico and Lithuania before official play even started. Then, in regular competition, they lost to the Argentinean team in the semifinals. The differences in salary were astronomical. The Americans were a multi-million dollar team of professionals who never had the time, or some say the motivation, to come together to play as a team. ESPN analyst Dick Vitale said of the team, "Let's learn from this disaster and unbelievable travesty. To think that basketball was founded by Dr. Naismith here in the States, and now we are no longer the dominant power; it is sad." Something good came out of the experience as American teams are once again emphasizing a team-based passing game rather than individual superstar dunking exhibitions.

INDIVIDUAL SPORTS VS. TEAM SPORTS

It's one thing to let yourself down; it's another to let your team down. A solo loss can be far harder to handle than a team loss where players have a built-in support system and teammates to help soften the blow. A baseball player wins or loses with his team, while a swimmer must face the clock alone. If your student-athletes are involved in swimming, wrestling, golf, skiing, equestrian, tennis, fencing or any other individual sport, try to get them to play in the context of a team and emphasize the team aspect of the sport. Individual scores add up to team wins or loses. Student-athletes should pay close attention to how their own performances will affect the team's win or loss. Encourage young athletes to help their fellow competitors rather than rival them. Good team players will do their personal best but also support their teammates to do the same. Children should develop a sense of reward and delight from seeing others succeed, whether they are teammates or opponents. Solo athletes should compete with a team mentality with a shared attitude and intention. Help your children see the benefits and rewards of the team structure.

Student-athlete, Sierra Paresi, High School Tennis Team

I think the difference between a real team sport like softball and individual competition sports like tennis is that in softball you all win or lose together, but in tennis there is more pressure because you are responsible yourself for how you play and behave. We have a really good coach who has taught us all to play and behave the same way, as a team. He tells us not to argue about line calls and to play an honest game. He says that it's better to lose honestly than win dishonestly. I think we all believe that, so it strengthens our team.

During one competition, we overheard another coach telling his team that if they were losing really badly, they could lie about the line calls. Everybody on my team agreed that that's not what teamwork is all about.

Teamwork for the Good of the Sport

True team players care about everyone on the team, and that goes beyond the athletes. Star quarterbacks need the water boys; little league teams need sponsors; every team needs score keepers, and no one is going to get to the game without the bus driver. Teach your children a sense of community with everyone who makes the game possible. As we've seen in professional sports in recent years, cheating and poor-faith negotiations can damage the reputation of a sport which hurts everyone involved with the game – on and off the field. When a high school team gets kicked out of championship play because of cheating or bad behavior, they let down the fans, administrators, and parents – not just themselves. Student-athletes have to be taught to respect everyone who makes the games possible. Once there is money involved, in the world of professional sports, the stakes go up. The National Hockey League walkout in 2005 left thousands of people out of work and fans without a game. The organization failed to negotiate as a team, so everyone suffered. Athletes need to learn how teamwork goes beyond the players on the field. I asked Tony Dungy of the Indianapolis Colts, about the importance he puts on teamwork.

NFL Coach Tony Dungy, Indianapolis Colts

The difference between winning and losing at the professional level is very small and that difference is usually how well the guys work together and what kind of team players you have. So the number one thing we look at when considering a new player is how they are going to fit in. We have a good group of guys and we want our new guys to fit in and be good members of the community. We have a tremendous responsibility to our young boys across the country and especially here in Indianapolis to show people that being a good athlete is not enough. So many boys look up to our players. We want our guys to be positive role models. I have teenage boys and I don't want them copying the wrong character traits. It's important to me and Mr. Irsay that we get high quality people as well as players.

Aude Aliquid Dignum.
"Dare Something Worthy"
~ 16ᵗʰ Century Latin

A TEAM PLAYER GIVES BACK

Teamwork means giving back to your sport. Your children can coach younger children, manage a team if they can't play, or help with a game involving older athletes. There are plenty of ways to show your children how to give back. Golf great Tiger Woods tells his protégés that early on his father taught him two words that have stuck with him throughout his career – "care" and "share". Although he is a singular sensation, he is a team player when it comes to the sport of golf. He gives back. His foundation provides athletic and academic opportunities for underprivileged youth. The Tiger Woods Foundation and Target Corporation partnered in 2000 to create *Start Something*, a program that encourages youth ages 8 to 17 to identify a specific personal desire or goal and begin taking steps towards achieving their dreams. (Learn more about the program at http://startsomething.target.com.) Encourage your children to start giving back at an early age. Use real examples and find role models.

Tennis great Billy Jean King could have rested on her millions, but she continued to fight for equality in her sport and for future tennis athletes by founding the Women's Tennis Association, the Women's Sports Foundation and World Team Tennis, well after her professional career was over. She said of the sport, "My dream has always been to provide equal opportunities for everyone and keep World Team Tennis social, competitive, entertaining and fun. World Team Tennis will be my greatest achievement, the very best I can give back to the game."

TEAM PLAY IS FUN

Teamwork is planned and practiced, but it is also creative. When teammates really trust each other, they can have a great time in competition. Encourage your student-athletes to connect with their teammates, and encourage respect and trust on and off the field. Later in life, these skills will benefit them in any profession they choose. Nobody works in a vacuum, and they are far more likely to succeed if they know how to work as a team.

Jack Welch, former CEO of General Electric Corporation, is known for his business coaching success. He promotes a concept that he calls "boundary less" behavior. In business the concept refers to breaking down barriers between departments, suppliers, and other companies, as well as personal walls of race or gender, to develop new ideas and to put teamwork ahead of individual egos. This concept applies to athletic teams in terms of searching for new ways to cooperate and work together. Help your children think creatively about team play. Is there somebody on their team who needs help or encouragement? Is there an opportunity to get to know players on other teams that they can learn from? Teamwork can be incredibly rewarding if you can get your children out of their own heads and reaching out to other players.

While teamwork should be about the whole team, there are also some magical moments when a few teammates click to create a team within a team. Your children may play positions that allow them to form a special bond with another player – catcher and pitcher, quarterback and receiver, doubles tennis partners or members of a relay track or swim team. These types of athletic relationships require trust, understanding and cooperation. The following are some great teams within teams from the past.

THE FOUR HORSEMEN

Quarterback Harry Stuhldreher, left halfback Jim Crowley, right halfback Don Miller and fullback Elmer Layden created this famous lineup in 1922 under the coaching of Notre Dame's Knute Rockne. In 1925 Rockne, the Four Horsemen and the Notre Dame Team ended the season with a perfect record of 10-0. None of the Four Horseman stood taller than 6 feet or weighed more than 162 pounds, but they were a legendary backfield. As a unit in 30 games, they only lost to one team, Nebraska, twice.

They got their nickname after they posed for a publicity picture with the four players on horseback. After graduation, the Four Horsemen all pursued coaching careers.

THE PITTSBURGH STEELERS' STEEL CURTAIN

A team within the '78 Steelers, the 'Steel Curtain' included four of the toughest defensive linemen ever to play the game. Mean Joe Greene, linebackers Joe Lambert and Jack Ham, and defensive back Mel Blount connected as athletes to form a team sensation. The 'Steel Curtain' defense allowed only 195 points in a 17-2 season. The Steelers two losses were by a total of 10 points. In the playoffs, they beat the Denver Broncos 33-10 and the Houston Oilers 34-5, and then beat Dallas 35-31 in Super Bowl XIII.

Extreme Denver Bronco Fan

The best teamwork I've ever seen was The Three Amigos of the 1980's Denver Broncos; they were everything that a football fan wants to see in a team. They enjoyed supporting each other and sharing the fame; they didn't hog the spotlight as individuals. They were a unit. In their case 1 + 1 + 1 didn't equal three, it was more like nine; they squared themselves. You couldn't get a Denver Broncos ticket back then. In fact, I had a friend who worked as a concession manager just so she could see the games. As a divorce attorney, there were many times that I saw Broncos season tickets as the sorest point of negotiations in a divorce settlement. I even had a few wills contested over the inheritance of tickets. It was crazy.

* *The Three Amigos were Mark Jackson, Vance Johnson and Ricky Nattiel.*

WHEN YOU DON'T MAKE THE TEAM

Teamwork is great once you are on the team but what if you don't make the team? It can be one of the toughest disappointments in your children's lives. When this happens, you just have to be there for them. It's no time for blame. The worst possible thing you can do is go along with your child's contention that they had an off day or others made it because they are someone's son or daughter. If your children don't make the team, use this as an opportunity. This isn't the last time your children will have to deal with this kind of disappointment. The day will come when they don't get into a school, get a particular job or get asked out by a certain someone. Teach your children to take the blow graciously and move on, work harder and try again.

Timmy Dance

When I was ten years old I tried out for a youth hockey all-star team. Only 15 – 20 players were going to be picked from around the league. I was nervous, but I assumed that I would be picked so I developed a cocky swagger after I made the first cut. My father made it a point to tell me about how professional sports are filled with egos and attitudes, showboating and taunting, and how true champions know how to win with class. Winning with class means respecting your adversary, being cordial and humble, and carrying yourself 'as if you have done this before'.

Celebration is okay. In fact, it's natural to feel superior after you've won. But just as it feels great to win, it is very difficult to lose. Winning with class shows that you understand the pains of defeat and do not intend to step on other players when they are behind. Your opponents will respect you much more if you control your emotions and show dignity, rather than rub their noses in it. My Dad told me to remain humble and just keep digging for perfection on the ice because as good as it feels to assume you have already made the team, you have not made it yet; it's not over.

I always tried to listen to my father's words even though I was a knuckle-headed kid who thought he knew everything. I kept working hard and kept my cocky mouth shut through the remainder of the tryouts. Finally, the last tryout was called and the final roster was announced.

The coaches had a box of all-star jerseys ready to be given out to the players. The players not selected were told to leave the ice immediately and hit the showers. I remember that day like it was yesterday - the coaches yelling names and giving out jerseys, the players clapping, the parents yelling and clapping.

I was told to hit the showers. I wasn't going to be an all-star. My heart dropped, and all my emotions came out at once. I cried my eyes out. I remember my dad was at the door when I got off the ice. He knew that it was the biggest setback in my life and he was there to console me.

I didn't understand why I didn't make the team. I couldn't have tried any harder. My dad talked to me about handling disappointments in life in general, not just in sports. He told me that the way I handled this situation would either make me closer to being either a man or a baby. I really didn't understand what he meant back then, but all I knew was at that time I never wanted to see the ice again. After some time past, my dad came to me and told me how proud he was of me and what a good a hockey player he thought I was. He also told me that I shouldn't quit but instead use the experience as motivation to try harder the next season.

My dad always told my brother and me that success is not the same thing as winning, and failure is not the same thing as losing. He told me if I didn't quit and I worked harder for next hockey season, starting the next day, then I would have truly won because I didn't give up. My Dad never wants to see me give up at anything.

"Its not whether you win or lose but how hard you try," he said to me. At the time I thought my father's words were pretty corny, but I listened and continued to work hard. The following year I made the all-star team and came in second in total points among all the players.

I will carry this experience with me for the rest of my life as I will always remember my dad at the door waiting to console me and give me a shoulder to cry on when I was down in the dumps. "Win-at-any-cost" and "quit when you're down" are words that I will never live by.

-I Love You Dad-

For my yoke is easy, and my burden is light.
~ Matthew 11: 30

Katie Johnson, Michigan State Spartans

Timmy Dance, Cathedral Prep High School

Chapter Six

Coaching

**While people are called by various titles such as "boss"
or "chief" or "mentor", the title "coach" carries with it
a special meaning of affection and admiration by those
who confer that title upon a person. Not everyone
bears the title "coach" for it is earned only by investing
one's own soul in the life of someone else.**
~ Father Scott Jabo

Your young athletes will most likely start off completely dependent on you as their first coach, and then by the time they are playing college sports you'll find yourself on the sidelines, literally. It's going to be your job to gradually step back and let other coaches take over. It's all a part of giving children roots and wings. Give your children a great start in sports and then know when to turn over the reins.

Personally, I found it very easy to turn my sons over to coaches when they were very young because I trusted my sons to show respect. I knew that they would listen to their coaches because I taught them the old-fashioned value of respecting one another and respecting authority. When we teach our children values and boundaries, it is much easier to turn them over to coaches and teachers. I was confident that all I had taught my sons at home would make them good students on and off the playing field.

We also have to make sure that our children have good instructors. I always paid close attention to how coaches and trainers related to my sons. Not everyone has the patience or ability to teach kids. Over the years, I have noticed a trend with youth coaches to treat eight-year-olds as if they are fourteen or fifteen. I don't believe this works. Coaches have a responsibility to know how to deal with the different age groups that they are coaching. They must learn how to communicate on an appropriate level to gain the student-athletes' trust and respect. If a coach goes out onto the practice field sounding and acting like a drill sergeant, young children are likely to be intimidated and tune out the coach's orders. The goal for young student-athletes is to learn and have fun. The coaches who have been most memorable to my sons are the ones who treated them as if they were their own children. They still speak about their favorite coaches to this day. A great coach's influence can last a lifetime. I asked Tony Dungy of the Indianapolis Colts, how he and his staff coach character development.

NFL Coach, Tony Dungy, Indianapolis Colts

It's by what we do. We can't just say 'you have to be good people and get into the community and give back' So it's by how we live our own lives and the standards that we set and we let them know that we are there for them. We have a great counseling program in terms of personal development and we bring in a lot of speakers. But the most important thing is that our veteran players and senior staff are always there with the door open to talk to the young players and help them out. We look for problems before they come up.

Encouragement is oxygen to the soul.
~ Harry Mackay

VERY YOUNG

I think that a parent or family member should be a child's first coach. When your children first pick up a bat and ball, a tennis racket or a hockey stick or even a deck of cards, you should be their guide. You must teach proper behavior and respect for the game. You lay the foundation for how your children will treat coaches in the future; you define what the child should expect from a coach. You are also teaching your children how to interact with future coaches. It's not just about what they learn; it's also about *how* they learn from you and other adults. There are plenty of peewee hockey and little league coaches out there who find themselves with five and six-year-olds who are un-coachable, because they don't know how to listen or follow rules. Teach your children to be good listeners and good sports.

COACHING FOR SUCCESS

If you start off coaching your children for success, they will be prepared to take direction from future coaches. Here are some basics to teach very young children in a game situation:

- Have fun
- Don't cheat
- Be a good sport
- Try your hardest

HAVE FUN

When sports get more serious as your children grow, make sure they continue to enjoy themselves. The best athlete is the one who still sees the fun in the game. If the game isn't enjoyable for your children, they aren't going to continue playing.

NO CHEATING

The most important thing that you can teach a very young child is that cheating is absolutely unacceptable. There is no fudging, no ignoring boundary lines or rules. Cheating is not allowed. As I said earlier in this book, my son's high school track coach, David Woodard, says to every student-athlete, "I don't coach cheaters." I challenge every parent reading this book to say to their young children, "I don't raise cheaters." Every sport has rules; they must be respected. You can keep it simple at an early age, but children must understand that rules are to be followed, not broken. Think of the athletes, business people and politicians who could have stayed out of trouble if they had just learned not to cheat.

BE A GOOD SPORT

Teach your children sportsmanlike conduct. If you teach them to follow your rules and adopt their own personal code of conduct, they will be far better prepared to question a coach or player who promotes or allows bad behavior. Student athletes must develop their own high standards and know when to question authority. Young children are well aware of the tantrums and 'meltdowns' of other children. No one at any age wants to play with people who put up a fuss when they make a bad shot or miss a pass. Ask your children how they feel about other children talking back to a coach or having a tantrum. Help your children *want* to be good sports. Show them that they will have more fun and more friends in the game if they behave. This is a small step to maturity that should be taken as early as possible.

Another side to good sportsmanlike conduct is learning to be respectful of the coach, the team and the opponent. Teach your young children to question their coach in an appropriate way. This process should be determined by the coach. Ask the coaches how they want to be communicated with, on and off the field. A rule that both parents and children need to follow is no back talking to anyone, ever. Respect the officials. Never, ever question an official, and don't you dare, as a parent, question an official in front of your children. Just don't do it!

Finally, a good sport is a good winner and a good loser. Teach your children to say "Good game", to teammates and opponents, win or lose. A good sport never makes excuses for a loss or flaunts a win.

TRY YOUR HARDEST

Another point of sportsmanlike conduct is showing a consistent effort. Some children stop trying if they are losing or if their heads aren't in the game. Teach your children that if they are going to be in the game, they have to try to do their best. Point out that one child with a poor attitude can ruin the game for the whole team. Sports are more fun and more challenging when everyone puts in a good effort.

> **The mediocre teacher tells. The good teacher explains.**
> **The superior teacher demonstrates. The great teacher inspires.**
> ~ *William Arthur Ward*

YOUTH SPORTS COACHING

As your children enter competitive sports, in a school or youth program, you are going to have to relinquish control to other coaches. Your children will have to follow *their* rules. Without interfering, you should understand their rules and expectations; my premise is that parents, students, coaches and officials must have guidelines if they are going to work together to have a successful season. If everyone is working from the same rules then misunderstandings and disagreements can be avoided. At the beginning of the season, talk to your children's coaches and ask them if they are going to share a 'code of conduct' with the students and parents. If so, tell them how much you appreciate the effort, and, if not, offer to provide one.

COACH RICH JESSUP

I've had the pleasure to get to know an exceptional coach, Rich Jessup, who is also a minister and an inspirational speaker. I met him at the Pro Sports Outreach Program basketball camp in Erie, Pennsylvania, where he is a director along with NBA champion Charlie Ward. Through this program and others, Rich has spoken to over a million student-athletes about the importance of character development, academic excellence and the ability to overcome disappointment.

Rich was an exceptionally talented, multi-sport athlete in college who seemed destined for a professional sports career, but he fell short in the NBA draft. With the support of his parents, he didn't miss a beat. He turned a disappointment into a positive and built a coaching career based on his athletic abilities and his gift of communication. Rich has worked in law enforcement, athletic coaching and religious ministries where he's seen the best and worst of people. Now he travels the country spreading a message of hope and encouragement to student-athletes through sports camps and programs.

When he speaks to students, he gets their attention with a one-man globetrotter-type performance drawing the youth in with his basketball skills. Then he challenges them to think about what they are going to make of their lives. While he coaches for athletic excellence, he stresses the need for academic achievement, integrity and discipline. His message to young people is that it doesn't matter how good they look on the outside or how much money they make, it's what's on the inside that counts.

I like his philosophy towards coaching. He commits to athletes and parents that everyone will play but only the best and the hardest workers will play when the going gets tough. He wants to inspire the athletes to work hard and the parents to see beyond their own children and support the team. When putting together a team, Rich avoids the individual superstars and prefers the athletes who are going to work hard and be team players. He also encourages his students to set goals and keep a journal to track their progress.

Rich is also the father of two fine athletes and has passed on the strong family support system that he received from his own parents, who never missed a game and encouraged him during times of disappointment.

Athlete – Bob Sanders – NFL Football Player
My Best Coach

The best coach I ever had was Joe Moore, at Cathedral Prep. He's since passed away. He came back to our high school as an assistant football coach after an amazing career at Notre Dame. He was an exceptional coach because he had so much knowledge about the game and he was well respected by other coaches. He helped bring our team from a 3-8 season to a state championship. Part of the reason that he was a great coach was that he taught us how to behave as men and handle ourselves outside of football. He taught me to respect myself and others and the game. Coach Moore was always there for me. He pushed me and he kept telling me that I could do it. I think what he taught me has stuck with me because now that I feel as if young people are watching me, I know it's important for people like me to do the right thing – in the way I play football and in how I live my life.

Working With Coaches When Things Go Wrong

No parent or child should put up with inferior or misguided coaching. You have to teach your children to stand up for their principles. If any coach asks student-athletes to compromise their standards, they should speak up in an appropriate way. If you as a parent have to confront a coach regarding policies or behavior, you should only do it in an appropriate setting, with the coach's supervisor present if possible. It should never be handled in public. Also, parents should avoid ganging up on a coach. Your behavior as a parent should reflect the behavior that you expect from your children and from your coach.

I interviewed Jim Thompson, an expert in the field of positive coaching. He has been teaching and coaching for over 20 years and in 1998 founded the *Positive Coaching Alliance*, a movement of parents, coaches and youth sports organizations dedicated to "transforming youth sports so sports can transform youth." Thompson believes that youth sports should be considered an integral part of children's character development. He sees the coach's role as crucial to that development. "Coaches and teachers of youth sports don't make a lot of money," Thompson said, "but what they do have is a chance to have influence and influence that lives on. Values come from succeeding, when success is defined as mastery rather than ego gratification."

Advice from Jim Thompson for parents dealing with coaches who encourage bad behavior:

"If a coach is teaching children bad behavior then parents have a responsibility to step in immediately. If a coach is dishonoring the game, parents need to show moral courage in that situation. We talk a lot about physical courage but this situation requires a greater type of bravery. Most of us want to stay in our comfort zone and not embarrass ourselves or our children. We don't want to stand out from the crowd. But there is a time for parents to speak up and say that 'it's not ok'.

"If a coach is doing something unethical, speak directly to the coach in private. Be sure to listen carefully to his or her response. You also have to speak to your children about the behavior and let them know that 'it's not ok'. If parents are silent then children assume that the parents endorse the behavior. Let them participate in the decision.

"Then, monitor the situation. If you don't get satisfaction and see a change in the coach's behavior, you can't be afraid to go to his or her supervisor which may be a school principal or a board of directors.

"At the Positive Coaching Alliance, we encourage preemption. Do all you can before the season begins to avoid difficult situations. As soon as you know who your children's coaches are, make early, positive contact. Tell them that you appreciate their commitment and tell them you are there to help if asked. Also, understand their stress level. Even if they don't seem to be under stress, believe me – they are. Early in the season, look for truthful things that you can comment on. You can say things like 'I really appreciate your commitment as a coach and that you start and end practice on time'. Let them know that you appreciate what they are doing. Later in the season if you have a problem, you are not going to them as a complaining parent; you are going to them as a concerned parent. So, the first contact you have with them should be positive. We call it filling the emotional tank. Observe a cooling off period after a bad situation. Take a day and cool off. Think about what's happened and sleep on it. When you do talk to the coach, explain as specifically as possible how you would like to see things change.

"Another situation that comes up with coaching is when a child is not thriving and is losing interest in a sport. The coach may not be doing anything wrong, but your child is not reaping the benefits of being on a team. What do you do? I recommend again that if you have filled the emotional tank early in the season, then when you go to the coach as a concerned parent, say something specific that he or she can take action on, like 'Lately, my daughter doesn't want to go to practice. Do you have any idea how we can work together to help her?' Then listen carefully to the suggestions.

"In my organization, we work with coaches to create an organizational culture. The win-at-any-cost mentality, which causes most problems, comes down from professional sports where it is the most important thing. By default, youth sports programs have adopted a professional sports mentality. We recognize that leaders of youth organizations have not been properly trained. For the most part, they are volunteers. They are usually just thinking about having enough coaches and making sure the parents don't go bananas. We encourage coaches to develop an organizational culture where honoring the game comes first. We convince them that they have a lot of power to influence young people. They also have the power to set expectations for the parents. "

To learn about Jim Thompson's organization, go to www.positivecoach.org and read about his experience coaching high school girl's basketball in *Shooting in the Dark: Tales of Coaching and Leadership.*

Timmy Dance
My Best Coach

I've been really fortunate to have some great coaches in my life, but my best coach was Scott Grack, my track coach in high school. He pushed me so hard and expected so much out of me that I couldn't help but learn to believe in my abilities because of him. A great coach's influence goes far beyond the playing field. I've taken his advice and memories of his encouragement into all areas of my life.

HIGH SCHOOL COACHING

Once your student-athletes enter high school, the time will come to decide whether or not to get serious about a sport. You and your children will have to decide how much time, money and effort will be spent on sports and if your children are going to try for a college scholarship. This is the time to really get to know your children's coaches. Help your children zero in on a coach who believes in their talent and will help take the young athletes to the next level, whether that is a specialized camp or an introduction to another coach or trainer. Just as there are certain teachers who inspire athletes' academic successes, there will also be special coaches who inspire them to go for greatness in sports. Remember: a high school coach can open doors that you as a parent can't.

Student-athlete – Chelsea Gordon –
NCAA Basketball Scholarship
University of Illinois

I started playing basketball because my older sister Tiffany played, and my first coach was my dad. It was good and bad. He was a lot harder on me than on the other players because of the emotional connection. When I was young, I had to separate his being my Dad from his being my coach, and it felt awkward when he reprimanded the other girls, but all in all it was good. He really was a great coach.

My most influential coaches were Bill and Carrie Palermo with the AAU – Athletic Amateur Union – Pittsburgh Bruins team. We had a great team and they really raised my level of play. I sprained my ankle at one point and lost all my confidence. I was out for about a month and a half. I would have quit if it hadn't been for the Palermos. They took time out of their schedules to help me, and they taught me that the game isn't about scoring but about watching and really understanding it. They taught me that I don't have to be better than my opponent, but I have to be smarter.

COACHING FOR COLLEGE RECRUITMENT

I asked football coach Barry Alvarez of the University of Wisconsin Badgers about what he looks for in a student-athlete during the recruiting process. He told me that he is looking for "coachable kids". We talked about Ron Dayne and Kevin Stemke, two players who went on to successful NFL careers.

Ron Dayne was brought to Alvarez's attention by a counselor in South Jersey. He was a gifted athlete and had an unusual body for the skill position that the coach envisioned him in. He was big and stocky and most would have chosen him for a fullback but Alvarez recognized his talent as a tailback. He had size, speed and explosion. They had studied him and his ability in field competition as a discus thrower which showed the type of explosion he had. When he showed up freshman year, he was 275 pounds but he had big bursts on the field. They got him up to college level competition freshman year, and he was playing by the 3rd game; in fact, he rushed over 2000 yards in his freshman year. His high school coaches had done an excellent job helping him develop his skills.

"Personally", Alvarez says, "he was a pleasure to coach because he is a very quiet unassuming person. He never wanted a lot of attention." Alvarez and Dayne hit it off immediately and maintained a great relationship through his time at Wisconsin. He would visit Alvarez daily to talk about football and about personal things. They still keep in touch today.

Kevin Stemke, a kicker, was very athletic for the position and he had a great personality. He was an outstanding soccer player and had obviously received excellent coaching in that sport. He walked in and took over punting. The Badgers moved their players to a private dorm their first year, away from the rest of the student body. The other students didn't accept the players. They just didn't get along, yet Kevin somehow got everybody together. He was very competitive, but he also got along with everybody. He was a guy people really liked to have around. He was very unusual for a kicker. He became a conduit between the regular students and athletes.

According to Coach Alvarez, "When I coach, I coach kids for life, not just for competition. I teach them that they have to be accountable for their actions and get them to work very hard. The NFL knows what they are going to get from our athletes, that they are going to be as good off the field as they are in the locker room. The NFL knows that our guys are never going to be a problem in the community."

COLLEGE-LEVEL COACHING

By the time your child is competing at the college level, your role will be off the field, as their biggest fan and supporter. Student-athletes become young adults and the apron strings need to be cut. It's time to listen to them and respond to their needs. If they have hopes of going on to professional sports or if they have Olympic dreams, you are there to support, not push. Your greatest responsibility is to make sure that your children maintain their grades, right up to the day they graduate.

Parent – Fred Rush – Father of Penn State Offensive Guard Charles Rush

We taught our son Charles to play his best at any level but never to focus on football or the NFL. His focus has always been on graduation. He is playing football *on the way to graduation.* I like what a Michigan coach said to him during a recruiting visit. He asked Charles if he ever thought about the NFL and Charles said "*Yes*". The coach said, "*Well DON'T*". The clear message is that players have to put academics first. I also like what basketball great Bill Russell says to young athletes. He tells them that if they get a sports scholarship, it is only for the purpose of graduating. He says, "You can play sports *on the way* to graduation, you can fall in love or join a fraternity *on the way* to graduation, but be clear that your goal is - - *graduation.*"

Presumably, your children wouldn't have made it to this point if they didn't respect their coaches, so you do the same. Be respectful of a coach's time. If you want to talk about something, first ask how the coach likes to be contacted, by phone, email or through an assistant. Always keep it brief, and don't question coaching skills or a child's in-play time, unless of course something is truly wrong. Be supportive, not antagonistic. The best support you can give a college coach is to be a respectful fan. Your behavior should reflect your expectations of the child and the coach.

**Cathy George, Coach, Michigan State University,
Division I Volleyball**

When I coach I try to exude all the qualities that I expect from my players, good decision making, honesty and integrity. I have had a lot of my athletes go on to coaching so I understand that I am not just a role model for them as athletes but also as potential coaches. I'm handing down an example of how to coach.

How we act as a team, focusing on doing the right thing, says a lot about us. I emphasize a strong work ethic and integrity in all the things we do. I can't control how the other team plays or behaves, so I don't think about it. I believe that coaches set a tone for the players and the fans. I don't argue with officials. I tell my team that we are going to get some bad calls, and the opponent will get some bad calls. We don't complain about it or blame losses on officiating. I think our players and fans respect the way we compete.

**If you don't go after what you want, you'll never have it.
If you don't ask, the answer is always no.
If you don't step forward, you're always in the same place.**
Nora Roberts

THE GREATEST COACHES

I've picked a few outstanding coaches for you and your student-athlete to learn about. Find your own role models, and talk with your children about what makes a great coach. I believe that a coach should promote character development and that includes learning self-discipline, sacrifice, teamwork and good sportsmanship. There have been many winning coaches that have promoted and displayed bad behavior. Woody Hayes and Bobby Knight both won a lot of games, but would you want your children to be coached by someone who physically strikes players or promotes violence against other players? Talk about it with your children.

Vince Lombardi, NFL Coach, Green Bay Packers (1959-1967)

He led the Green Bay Packers to three consecutive NFL championships. He was great because of his dedication to his sport, his team and to proving his own coaching abilities. He demanded 110% effort and obedience from his players. Best known for his inspirational words, he was one of the greatest motivators of all time.

John Wooden – NCAA Baskeball Coach

"Failure to prepare is preparing to fail." Coach Wooden believed first and foremost in preparation for basketball and for life. During his 27 years he had a winning percentage record of 81.3, winning 10 NCAA championships, including seven in a row from 1967 – 1973. To learn more about coach Wooden, read one of his many books, including: *My Personal Best: Life Lessons from an All-American Journey.*

James Doc Counsilman – US Olympic Men's Swimming Coach

"The minute your curiosity dies, you're finished as far as any creative effort is concerned." 'Doc' Counsilman was head coach for the two most successful US Olympic Swimming Teams, in1964 and in 1976 when his team won 12 of the possible 13 gold medals. His dedication to the sport went beyond coaching. He studied the science of swimming and, through careful research, dramatically revised swimming methods. He published over 100 scientific papers on various aspects of competitive swimming.

Brutus Hamilton - University of California, Berkeley, Track Coach

Coach Hamilton was an outstanding athlete himself, winning silver in the 1920 Olympic decathlon, and placing sixth in the pentathlon. He also won the National AAU in both events earlier that year. He continued his dedication to the sport as coach at University of California and as Olympic head coach for the 1952 U.S. Track Team. His athletes set two world records and seven Olympic records, and he led his college team to seven titles. His Olympic athletes included Hall of Fame sprinter Harold Davis, pole vaulter Guinn Smith and middle-distance runner Don Bowden, who was the first American to break the four-minute mile.

THE COACHES COACH

Coaches rarely work in a vacuum. They work for schools or private programs with administrators or boards of directors. The administrators who hire coaches set personal expectations and performance levels that reflect their own professional goals as well as the goals and mission of the school or program. Try to understand the pressures that your children's coaches may be under from their bosses. Hopefully, the coaches and their managers or directors are in sync when it comes to the well-being of your children. If you suspect that your children's coaches are getting mixed messages or negative direction from 'higher-ups", ask questions. Your child's sports program administrators should be able to communicate their mission and philosophy.

Father Scott Jabo, headmaster of Cathedral Prep High School in Erie, Pennsylvania
A coach is much more than a person who is out to win games or who knows the X's and O's of playing a sport, as important as that is to a degree. A coach is a person who can tap into the inner spirit of an athlete and motivate that athlete to accomplish much more than he ever thought possible both on and off the field. The coaches I want at our school are those who can see athletics in its proper perspective, that is, as part of an overall program to develop the whole person in spirit, mind, and body. They must genuinely care about the athletes entrusted to their care and also recognize the great responsibility they have to form these athletes properly. Great coaches know the influence and impact that they have on their athletes and, as such, will use that power to influence each athlete to be a better person overall. I look for coaches who are people of integrity and strong moral

character, who posses a passion for what they do and who can inspire their athletes to be and do the same. I value coaches who can teach and instill values such a teamwork, commitment, discipline and good sportsmanship in their athletes so that their athletes will carry those same qualities with them for the rest of their lives and in every situation. If I find anything less than that in a person, I will not hire him to coach our athletes. Thus, I place very high importance on selecting the right kind of coach for our athletes, for the relationship that an athlete has with his coach will impact him for the rest of his life.

A FINAL WORD ON COACHES

I hope that parents and student-athletes will take a fresh look at the importance and impact that great coaches have in your lives. I hope you support them, appreciate them and talk them up in your community. It's all too easy to dump on coaches when they aren't perfect, and no one is perfect. A great coach can change lives and schools and communities for the better. That is a lot of power. I urge parents and student-athletes to let their feelings be known. Be respectful and praise your great coaches.

Jere Johnson, the Northwest Suburbs Director of the Greater Chicago Fellowship of Christian Athletes

In 1986, I was the youngest varsity basketball coach in the State of Indiana. I studied older coaches to gain knowledge and wisdom. One area I should have paid attention to was how they knew when to talk and when to keep their mouths shut. Of course, as a young coach I had to learn the hard way. I think I got more than 10 technicals my second year of coaching. None of them were for bad language, but all were for failing to keep my mouth shut at the right times. After each "T," I would ask myself, "When am I going to learn?"

Solomon (the author of Proverbs) knew quite well that there was a time for speaking and a time to just keep his yapper shut! Many people today need to learn that lesson. Some people mean well, but their lips keep moving when their ears should be listening. So many times they "open mouth, insert foot." However, if the mouth never opens, the foot stays where it belongs.

I would love to tell you that I mastered the art of keeping my mouth shut at the right times in my coaching, but, alas, I'm still working on it. But I have realized that when I do keep it shut I get into far less trouble with officials, parents, players and even my wife.

There is great wisdom in keeping quiet. No wonder some of the smartest people I know never say a word. Lesson learned. . . I hope! Jere can be found at www.sportsdevo.com.

**There is not enough darkness in all the world
to put out the light of one candle.
~ Robert Alder**

Coach Mike Mischler

Coach Kirk Ferentz,
Iowa Hawkeyes

Coach Kathy George, Michigan State Spartans

Chapter Seven

Competing

If you want to be incrementally better: Be competitive.
If you want to be exponentially better: Be cooperative.
~ Unknown

A star athlete is a great competitor. But what does it mean in our current culture to be a great competitor? Over the years, I've seen first hand, the tragic decline of standards in sports on behalf of parents, coaches and athletes. Winning has become the only goal of competition. It is a broken value that pushes athletes and coaches to cheat rather than risk losing. We have to turn the tide, and I think that the only way to do it is to talk about it. It's a discussion that must take place in the media and over dinner tables and involve experts and athletes, program administrators and sports officials. We have to stand up and battle the 'win at any cost' mentality that is destroying our youth. Let's teach our kids that competition is much more than winning.

In seeking answers as to why competition has gone wrong and in trying to find out how we can change things, I talked to two renowned sports psychologists, Dr. Alan Goldberg and Jerry Lynch, Ph.D. Without knowing that the other had done the same, they both started their discussions with me by pointing out that the Latin derivation of *competition* is 'to seek together.' This is a very important point; competition is not about annihilating the opponent or fighting one another but rather about cooperating with each other to play a game with the maximum level of skill and sportsmanship.

Alan and Jerry also agree that competition has become something ugly. Competition has evolved in our culture to become something antagonistic rather than cooperative.

Dr. Goldberg, who is the founder of Competitivedge.com, says that the problems with competition in youth sports today are caused by adults who are not doing their jobs. Dr. Goldberg says, "Some adults believe that youth sports are all about winning and when that happens, our kids are compromised."

Sports Psychologist - Dr. Alan Goldberg, Competitivedge.com

On coaches: "Unfortunately, the coaches who are ignoring poor sportsmanship are the least likely to listen to feedback from parents. But I think that parents have a responsibility to step in and confront these coaches – at the appropriate time and place. I recommend that parents never talk to a coach right before, during or after a game. The coach is under too much pressure and is too distracted. When you do talk to coaches and don't get results, then you have to go to their administrators."

On officials: "Limits need to be set by officials. If a coach is confronting an official, then the official has got to be very clear about the consequences and follow through with them. I refer to officials as one of the 'uncontrollables'. When athletes focus on an uncontrollable, they make themselves nervous and that undermines confidence."

On parents: "I think parents need to be trained, and it must be formalized training. We make an assumption that adults will behave in a mature way. Not so. Sports are evocative and can bring out the ugly side of anyone. I recommend that parents be given guidelines before the season starts. It's not enough to send a piece of paper home to be signed. There should be a meeting where conduct is discussed and consequences are presented. Parents should be considered a part of the team."

Sports Psychologist - Jerry Lynch Ph.D. Founder TaoSports

Parents and coaches are putting too much pressure on athletes to win. Parents are internalizing their children's wins and living through them. Sports, especially at the youth level, should be about learning the values of competition that will be used later in life, not about winning.

I try to teach athletes a functional relationship with their sport. I teach them that they should embrace their competitor and enjoy the competition. The better one's competitor is, the greater the challenge. It's through contest (testing each other) that we find out how good we really are. I also teach athletes and coaches to look differently at losing. Losing is inevitable. Unfortunately in western society, losing is considered abominable. We have moved to a 'win at any cost mentality', to a point where athletes will cheat rather than lose.

I'm influenced by eastern thinking and a belief that it is through losing that we win. We win when we experience loss because that is where we learn and become stronger. I share with my athletes that my successes are all based on what I have learned from loss and rejection.

Embrace your competitor as your partner and if you lose, accept the lessons the experience offers you.

Teaching Your Children to Be Good Competitors

No matter what your children's ages, you can teach them or remind them how to be a good competitor. Keep it simple. It's all about preparation and focusing on the details of the process and not the outcome. Your children should concentrate on training, knowledge of the sport and execution of skills and teamwork during the game – NOT THE SCOREBOARD.

Focus On:

Training	Put in the time to mentally and physically prepare for competition.
Skills	Learn, practice and demonstrate the skills needed for competition.
Knowledge	Study the game and learn from coaches and fellow athletes.

| **Behavior** | Show sportsmanlike conduct at all times. Follow the rules. |
| **Teamwork** | Cooperate and work with teammates, coaches and officials |

These are all things that athletes can control. By focusing on doing their personal best, student-athletes will become great competitors.

WHAT NOT TO FOCUS ON:

The Scoreboard	Focus on performance not the scoreboard.
Officials' Calls	Don't argue with a referee – EVER.
The Weather	You can't do anything about it. Deal with it.
Parents and Fans	Keep your head in the game, not in the stands.

These same skills can be applied to test-taking, interviewing for a job, giving a presentation or planning an event. It all comes down to staying focused on the task at hand and not looking around for external forces that will distract.

Another expert I've had the pleasure of speaking with on the subject of competition is Jim Rimmer, the Director of Operations at the Family First Sports Park in Erie, Pennsylvania. He is also a past national champion in martial arts and has been a minister for thirty-five years. He has a unique perspective as both a pastor and an athletic coach, but as he sees it, they go hand in hand. Jim says that he teaches to the trinity of mind, body and spirit. All three have to be trained for optimum performance in sports. Jim teaches children that resilience is also an essential element for success. He says that it is only through the ability to bounce back from losing and from life's other disappointments that we can truly develop as people. Jim believes that resilience comes from faith: in oneself, in God, in one's team and in one's sport.

He recently had three of his martial arts students go on to national competition, and he told them that they would need to call on their faith for the mental and spiritual toughness to meet the higher level of competition. Jim believes that the rewards of winning bring an additional stress of meeting tougher competition and that new stress should not be overlooked or taken lightly.

Jim said, "I didn't even want my three athletes to think about the national level of competition. I trained them the way the army trains parachutists. Parachutists focus on their gear and their jump routine and not on the fact that they are going to jump out of a plane. I get my athletes to focus on what they are supposed to be doing in the moment and away from the competition and prospect of winning."

> **[The most fun thing is] getting out there and mixing it up with friends; it's the competition.**
> *~ Al Unser, Jr.*

Winning Isn't Everything

Losing is as significant as winning. It's not something to lament over; it's an opportunity to learn and bounce back and be stronger. Losing is not failing. It helps create balance. Sports are a great way to build self-confidence and awareness, which will help build self esteem. I think student-athletes should have a winning attitude in order to be able to compete effectively, but not have a win-at-any-cost attitude. This attitude results in athletes sacrificing their integrity, trust, relationships, careers, and even marriages, as many professional athletes have experienced. Losing has helped my children develop into well-adjusted adults. They work hard daily at winning in all that they do but not at any cost. They realize that at times, they will fall short in their ventures, but understand that the balance of winning and losing has prepared them for what is ahead in life.

**The ultimate victory in competition is derived from the
inner satisfaction of knowing that you have done your
best and that you have gotten the most out
of what you had to give.**
~ Howard Cosell

In high school, my younger son Tommy, a two-time State champion in the 110 high hurdles and national qualifier, lost in a track meet to his biggest competitor. He was hurt and, in a way, embarrassed. He took it very hard, and before I knew it, I had a 6'2", 195-pound star athlete crying in my arms. When he first started the race, he was leading by almost an arm's length. He actually led up to the last two hurdles and in record time. Unfortunately for him he clipped a hurdle and did everything he could just to prevent himself from falling to the ground. Later, losing this track meet proved to be the best thing that could have happened to him. I knew right away that the moment was much bigger than the loss; it was a moment that would change Tommy's whole outlook. In a strange way, I don't think he would have been prepared to face his next challenge, the State track meet, if it hadn't been for this loss. All season long, he was under a great deal of pressure because he was the defending state champion. He was not only a target for his competitors, but fans and spectators expected him to win. I believe this loss relieved him of the pressures and expectations and allowed him to relax and re-focus on the bigger picture. Tommy went on to win at the state track meet.

Tommy learned how to come back bigger, stronger, and faster - mentally, physically, and spiritually. He will carry this lesson with him the rest of his life. We both believe that it was God's will. I believe that having a strong Christian background has helped us get through many difficult moments in athletics and in all life's challenges. It has helped us to put things into perspective. No matter what one's religion or spirituality, there are times when athletes have to look outside themselves and draw inspiration from something bigger. Athletic stars have to believe that they have the ability and the will to compete at a higher level.

Setbacks to Success

- 1832- Lost job
- 1833- Failed in business
- 1835- Sweetheart died
- 1836- Had nervous breakdown
- 1838- Defeated for State Speaker
- 1843- Defeated for nomination for Congress
- 1848- Lost re-nomination for Congress
- 1854- Defeated for U.S. Senate
- 1856- Defeated for nomination for Vice President
- 1858- Again defeated for U.S. Senate

In 1860 President Abraham Lincoln was elected President of the United States; during his presidency slavery was abolished and our nation was saved. A great competitor never gives up.

LOVE OF THE GAME

If we teach our children that winning is everything, we are doing them and ourselves a huge disservice. When children fear failure, they lose creativity and they look to cheating and violence to ensure a win. The best way to combat fear of failure is to teach your children a love of their game and a love of competition. Take the focus off the outcome and put it on the process. Life's a journey! Learning to be a good competitor starts at home with teaching the basic fundamentals of religion, respect, honor, discipline and integrity. Only a tiny percentage of student-athletes will make a living from sports. The majority of student-athletes will make a living at something else, and their sports scores won't matter. What will matter is that they have learned good sportsmanship, teamwork and personal commitment. Those are the attributes that will ensure success.

Jeff Catrabone – University of Michigan – Former Wrestler – Wrestling Coach - University of Buffalo

When I think about winning, I think about the rewards of the preparation. My father taught me to win like a man and lose like a man. I never liked to lose; who does? But as I grew older, I learned *how* to lose. When I was young and lost, I got angry. I would get mad at everyone and blame others for my failure. But through the years my father taught me there is no one to blame but myself and to take responsibility for my own actions. I have learned that losing is usually due to a lack of preparation, and if I work harder, I'll be less likely to lose the next time.

It took a long time to understand the consequences of throwing temper tantrums. People don't want to play with a bad sport. When you are older, it is even more important to be a good loser. That's how you earn respect. I earned a full wrestling scholarship to the University of Michigan and became one of the winningest wrestlers in their history with 160 wins and 55 pins. I was a three-time All American and a three-time Big Ten runner up. I knew that other athletes looked to me as a role model. I took my sportsmanship very seriously as an example for others.

Now as a coach at the University of Buffalo, I am preparing other young men to be the best they can be at their sport; I want them to win, but not at any cost. I push them hard and prepare them mentally and physically for competition. I am very serious about cheating, whether it's breaking rules or using drugs. I feel that if you need to cheat to win, it will eventually break you mentally. I teach my athletes that if they do everything the right way and train as hard as they can, then they will succeed, mentally and physically.

Great competitors know the rules and play by them. There is nothing wrong with questioning officials if one believes that the rules have been violated. Unfortunately, some competitors handle this irrationally by talking back to officials and yelling at opponents. It just isn't necessary. Great competitors know how to keep their cool and approach officials in a rational manner.

Stephone Beason, PIAA High School Basketball Official

I referee JV High School basketball. To get my official's license, I had to study and take a test on rules, regulations and codes of conduct. I clearly understand my role on the basketball court, but I have been surprised at the lack of respect that parents, coaches and students have for officials and our purpose. One of the worst cases I've seen was during a 3rd and 4th grade game. Two players ran into each other, the coaches started going off on each other and then went after the other referee on the court. The other referee had to kick one of the coaches out of the gym, so the coach pulled his own son, who was playing on his team, out of the game. In one of the programs I officiate, we read a code of conduct out loud before each game to try and prevent problems like this, but, obviously, more needs to be done about parents' lack of respect for officials.

Great competitors never play the blame game. One thing that I have made very clear to my sons is that they never, under any circumstances, blame anyone or anything for their losses. That is a life lesson that will serve your children well in their adulthood. Children have to face the fact that life isn't fair. That's what makes life so interesting. That's what makes life wonderful. We have to compete to get what we want. We compete in school, in games, in business and in relationships. How we compete will determine our success and our level of happiness. Teach your children to compete well, by the rules, with knowledge, skill, humor and, most importantly, a spirit of cooperation.

Overheard at an 8th grade girl's softball game.

Student-athlete: "What's the score?"

Coach: "What does it matter?"

Student-athlete: "I want to know if I need to try harder."

Chapter Eight

The Darker Side of Sports

"I told him, 'Son, what is it with you?
Is it ignorance or apathy?'
He said, 'Coach, I don't know and I don't care."
~ Frank Layden, Utah Jazz President,
on problems with a former player.

Ignorance and apathy are the enemies of a student-athlete. I ask you, please, to teach your children to know and care about the challenges they will inevitably face on the playing field and in life. Give your children the knowledge and strength to handle hard times and make tough decisions.

Your children are going to suffer hurt and loss in their lives. They are going to lose games and friends; they may have serious injuries, and they will have many disappointments. Rather than shielding them, or putting blinders on them, we can teach them how to handle the hurt and get through the healing process. We can teach them how to bounce back with grace, and with some understanding of what's happened so they can learn and grow from their experiences. Teach your children how to make good decisions and avoid self-destructive behavior. I truly believe that God doesn't give us anything that we can't handle. But we must *learn* how to handle the problems we are going to face.

The ' win at any cost' attitude that is pervasive in sports and in society sets our children up for an unrealistic expectation that everything should always go their way. Failure and loss are facts of life that must be faced head on and dealt with. The good news is that your children will learn far more from their failures than their successes. If young children learn how to handle small disappointments, they will be far better prepared for the bigger ones later in life.

I think that the toughest challenges our student-athletes face are violence, drugs, peer pressure and cheating. These are the short-cuts that tempt athletes in their pursuit of victory. You have to know these enemies, be able to recognize them, confront them and then take action. You can't educate your children until you educate yourself. A bottle of pills that you think are vitamins may be anabolic steroids. A bruise that you think came from football practice may have come from a violent hazing incident. Coaches may be telling your children that cheating is ok. If you don't know what's going on, you can't do anything about it.

When you talk to your children, it isn't going to be enough to tell them what drug abuse is; you need to paint a vivid picture of the consequences of drug abuse. It's the same with all of these challenges – talk about consequences, give real–life examples. Read the papers, listen to the news and talk to your children about the hard facts of life.

CHEATING

The temptation to cheat starts at a young age when children realize how easy it is to call a ball out when it's in or move a game piece a few extra spaces on a board. Cheating must be confronted when it happens. There must be real and consistent consequences, or it can develop into a habit. Turning your back on cheating is the same thing as condoning it.

If children learn that they can win if they cheat at cards when they are five years old, and aren't corrected, they may continue the behavior. When they are twelve, they may cheat on a test. At sixteen, they might cheat in soccer to win an important game. In college, they might cheat on a term paper to get their diploma. Then when they are an adult, they might illegally adjust accounting figures in their businesses. The consequences are then serious and, if they get caught, it won't be a time out in their room, they will go to jail. Look around. It happens all the time.

Cheating is an easy way to win – it's a quick fix. Consider the number of corporate executives who have chosen to cheat and lost everything. Consider the professional athletes who have also lost everything because of cheating. It's not a victimless act. Too often an entire team pays the price for one cheating teammate. An entire company goes bankrupt because of one executive's action.

What are the consequences of cheating?
Academic failure, getting kicked off a team,
social failure, financial ruin, jail time

For the student-athlete there are two kinds of cheating to be concerned with: academic and athletic. Student-athletes, school administrators and coaches across the country often bend the rules, to a point of breaking, when it comes to academic eligibility.

ACADEMIC DISHONESTY

If your children are paying others to do their work or cheating on tests in order to stay on a team, put a stop to it. If your children's coaches are assisting in academic cheating, do something about it. If you look at a college that has an unusual academic exemption policy for athletes, check into it. Your children are going to college to graduate, not to cheat themselves out of an education for the faint promise of a professional athletic career. When coaches or institutions turn a blind eye to cheating, your children are being cheated. If your children get away with cheating, they will carry the message for the rest of their life that cheating is ok as long as you get away with it, as long as you win, as long as you make money. Take action against academic cheating. Teach your children to value their education.

Academic cheating and academic exemptions are rampant in higher education. Some schools have extreme academic exemptions allowing athletes to play while failing to meet normal academic requirements. The athletes may get to play, but they aren't learning and most likely won't graduate. It doesn't make sense. Let's say that your student-athletes are some of the best and they go onto professional sports to become the next Tom Bradys or Tiger Woods. They are going to be in the spotlight and make a lot of money. Don't you want them to be able to handle the fame and the fortune to benefit themselves and others? Without an education, the rest is meaningless.

Some colleges have graduation rates under 25% for their athletes. However, the tide seems to be turning. In 2005, the NCAA started evaluating a new system – APR, Academic Progress Rate. With this new system, an athlete must have 40 percent of the degree requirements fulfilled after two years, 60 percent after three years and 80 percent after four years. If individuals on the team don't meet the criteria, scholarships will be in jeopardy.

ATHLETIC CHEATING

Parents must teach children how to play by the rules. It's easy to cheat. Cheating will always be an option, so we have to raise children who choose not to cheat. There have been plenty of coaches, high school and college, exposed for advocating cheating. It is up to you as a parent to monitor the behavior of your children's coaches. If you see cheating, confront it in an appropriate manner. A twelve-year-old horseback rider told me about a trainer who advocated that riders accuse their competitors of false violations. I asked her if the parents knew about it. She told me that they did but didn't say anything. Fortunately the child spoke up, and the trainer was exposed.

If your children are caught cheating or admit to it, deal with it immediately. Use it as an opportunity. Help them learn from their mistakes.

Let's honor our mistakes by allowing them to teach us.
Let's consider our failings to be gifts, and share them
humbly with others. Let the cracks in our perfect
facades let in light and air so that new life
can grow through them.
~ Molly Gordon

DRUG ABUSE

For a generation steroid use has been one of sport's dirty little secrets, from high schools to the pros. Two thousand and five was a watershed year with an unlikely whistleblower turning the spotlight on performance enhancement drugs. Ex-baseball player Jose Conseco admitted to taking steroids and helping others take steroids. Because of Conseco's admission and the embarrassing denials on the part of other baseball players, professional sports organizations are now dealing with steroid use. The fines are bigger and are now being enforced. Now it's time for parents to talk about steroid use, expose it and deal with it. Confront coaches and trainers who allow your children to use steroids in order to win.

A mother in Texas bravely took on a coaching staff and school administration when she learned that her son and his football team were taking steroids with the approval of a coach. She didn't accept the lies or cover-ups and persevered until the coach admitted his part in the steroid use. It was an incredibly brave act that should serve as an example to others. That woman probably saved the lives of many young men.

Steroid use doesn't just threaten the life of the athletes taking the drugs but also other athletes. Steroid use often leads to excessive rage and violence, endangering those who come in contact with the athletes. It is not a victimless crime.

What are the ultimate consequences of drug abuse?
Illness, irreversible disabilities, violence,
financial ruin, jail time, death

I've purposely printed the next two identical pages with information about the possible side effects of anabolic steroid use. Please rip out one of the pages and put it on your refrigerator door, or in your child's bathroom next to the mirror. Steroid use affects everyone differently, but the worst case scenarios are life threatening.

Anabolic-androgenic steroids are man-made drugs that are prescribed for men with health risks associated with abnormally low amounts of testosterone. Abuse of these drugs can lead to liver tumors and cancer, jaundice (yellowish pigmentation of skin, tissues, and body fluids), fluid retention, high blood pressure, increases in LDL (bad cholesterol) and decreases in HDL (good cholesterol). Other side effects include kidney tumors, severe acne, and psychiatric problems.

Some athletes abuse anabolic steroids to improve performance and physical appearance. Anabolic steroids are taken orally or are injected. 'Cycling' of steroids refers to the practice of taking the drugs for a period of time and then going off the drug for a period of time. There are many different types of vitamins, supplements and drugs that are available for athletes. Some are safe, some are questionable and some have life threatening side effects. As a parent, you need to be informed.

Side Effects of Anabolic Steroid Use

For Girls:

- Facial hair, deep voice, increased body hair, irregular periods, increased appetite, enlarged clitoris

For Boys:

- Increased breast size, shrunken testicles

For Both:

- Severe acne, baldness, liver abnormalities, and tumors, angry outbursts ("roid rage") or aggressive behavior, paranoia, hallucinations, psychosis, blood clots

Look in the mirror and PICTURE THIS:

If you are a girl on steroids – You are fat, balding and have to shave your face. You speak with an unusually deep voice, you have angry unexplained outbursts, exhibit paranoid psychotic behavior and you are in danger of dying from liver disease or blood clots and – oh, you also have severe acne!

If you are a boy on steroids – You have severe acne on your face and back, you have oily skin and are losing your hair. Your testicles have shriveled up and your breasts are growing. You have unexplained outbursts of anger and exhibit paranoid psychotic behavior. When you aren't hallucinating, you are obsessing over the fact that you could drop dead of a blood clot at any moment.

SIDE EFFECTS OF ANABOLIC STEROID USE

For Girls:

- Facial hair, deep voice, increased body hair, irregular periods, increased appetite, enlarged clitoris

For Boys:

- Increased breast size, shrunken testicles

For Both:

- Severe acne, baldness, liver abnormalities, and tumors, angry outbursts ("roid rage") or aggressive behavior, paranoia, hallucinations, psychosis, blood clots

Look in the mirror and PICTURE THIS:

If you are a girl on steroids – You are fat, balding and have to shave your face. You speak with an unusually deep voice, you have angry unexplained outbursts, exhibit paranoid psychotic behavior and you are in danger of dying from liver disease or blood clots and – oh, you also have severe acne!

If you are a boy on steroids – You have severe acne on your face and back, you have oily skin and are losing your hair. Your testicles have shriveled up and your breasts are growing. You have unexplained outbursts of anger and exhibit paranoid psychotic behavior. When you aren't hallucinating, you are obsessing over the fact that you could drop dead of a blood clot at any moment.

Those 'pictures' of steroid use may seem a bit extreme, but they are all proven side effects. Your children's health comes first but appealing to their vanity may be a more effective way to reach them.

The following is a true story that was told to me by a man who lived a steroid nightmare. In just a few years he went from a typical middle-class teenager, playing football and working out in a neighborhood gym, to facing a drug conviction that led to over four years in a federal penitentiary. This is a true story. Do not let this happen to your child.

A Steroid Story: Anonymous

I came from an upper middle class family. I went to a prep school and had many advantages in life. I was an all-round good athlete and first string on my basketball, football and soccer teams in middle school. In the summer of my 8th grade year, I started working out at our local YMCA. Nautilus machines were popular and I saw good results from working out three to four times a week. The strength training definitely improved my athletics. By my senior year in high school, I was about 6 feet tall and 185 pounds, and I decided to join a free weight lifting club at a local gym. I was really naïve about the whole weight lifting world. I was just taking vitamins and protein powders at that point.

At the gym I ran into a kid I knew who was a few years older than I was, and he had gotten huge, very muscular. He'd been down to Florida for a while, and I couldn't believe the change in him. I commented on his physique, and he asked me "Are you taking any gear?" I had no idea what he was talking about. We walked to his apartment where he asked me if I wanted to look like a bodybuilder and, of course, I said yes. He sold me 10 syringes of steroids and told me how to inject them. He also sold me some pills. At the time I thought nothing about the danger. All I knew was that I wanted the size.

My first cycle of steroids was 12 weeks long and was the most effective because my body was clean. My results were dramatic. Using 300 milligrams a week, in barely three months my bodyweight jumped from 185 pounds to 220 pounds and my bench press increased by 50 lbs and several reps. It was ridiculous. I felt like I grew everyday. Suddenly I was in the fold; I was one of the guys at the gym. I just told my parents that I was eating more and in a new training program. They didn't know anything about steroids, so they didn't suspect anything.

I was feeling big and strong and invincible. They call it the 'Superman Syndrome'. I felt amazing. I didn't want to go out partying with my friends any more; and while there was no 'buzz' from steroids I got such a mental high from the lifting that it was all I wanted to do. In this first 12 week cycle I didn't have any side effects like acne or hair loss. The only thing I saw was some minor testicular atrophy. I talked to the guy I bought the drugs from, and he told me not to worry, that it was only a temporary side effect

At the end of the cycle when the drugs ran out, I didn't really feel different right away because it takes several weeks for steroids to leave your body. A few weeks later, however, I started noticing that I wasn't recovering as quickly from my workouts and I was looking softer, not as pumped up. I didn't intend to go back for more and it had nothing to do with the cost. The cost of a steroid cycle was comparable to what I would normally spend in the same time at the local vitamin store. But I was losing size and strength; my weight settled down at about 200 pounds, and I was struggling to bench press around 300 pounds. Even though I had net gains from where I started, I was judging myself from my peak weight and performance while I was doing the drugs. I was comparing my natural body to an unattainable standard.

I went back to the same guy for more. Because he didn't see anything wrong with it, I didn't see anything wrong with it. I was just another guy trying to be a bodybuilder. You see it in every small town – there is always at least one hardcore gym where bodybuilders compete, and that's where you get your steroids. My second dose didn't give me the same big effect because my body had acclimated to the drugs. My friend explained that I needed more of the drug to get a similar effect. 'Up the dose' is the mantra. I went through the second cycle and I was 100%

hooked. I just wanted to get bigger. I felt deceptively healthy because I wasn't eating junk food or drinking alcohol. All I did was eat, work, and exercise. It became obsessive. By using more drugs, the side effects did start to hit me. I started to experience more severe testicular atrophy; I wasn't sleeping well from all the extra testosterone in my body, and I was getting the oily skin and acne. At that point, while I knew it was illegal, I had no idea what the penalty was if I got caught. All I could see was the short-term satisfaction.

Things got bad when I started to experience the down times in between cycles. It's a terrible time. You feel depressed and don't want to train. You can't lift as much. Everybody is supposed to stay off for several months between cycles but it's tough. I started seeing that every time I went back on steroids I'd have to take more and more to get the same effect. I went along like this for years treating steroids like a daily vitamin. After about four years my gym closed and I got in with another crowd. These guys were at a whole other level. Whereas before I was buying from 'buddies', now I was buying from regular dealers and hardcore competitive bodybuilders. They taught me new tricks like 'stacking' or combining different kinds of steroids. These were the kinds of guys who actually drove to Mexico to buy the stuff, along with other drugs. At this point I was a solid 240 pounds and I was doing 2000 milligrams of steroids to get the same effect that I had from 300 milligrams in the beginning.

My drug use expanded from steroids to other drugs, like Valium to help me sleep and other drugs to help between steroid cycles to offset the negative side effects. One of the dealers I bought from got busted and I got scared. I left my regular non-fitness job and moved to Florida, convinced I could become a fitness trainer at a big name gym. It only took a few days before someone approached me and asked me if I had enough 'gear'. Southern Florida is crazy; it was a whole new level of steroid dealing. It's not back room; it's rampant. I walked out to the guy's car, and he sold me $800 worth of steroids out of his trunk. And everybody is bigger in Florida. At 240 pounds, I felt small again. I 'upped the dose' to 3500 milligrams and also started taking growth hormone drugs. The combination took me from 240 pounds to nearly 290 pounds within two years. I wanted to enter a bodybuilding competition but never thought I was big enough. I'd say 'just ten more pounds and I'll be ready....' At this point I was starting to have some episodes of uncontrollable rage. Not all of the time, but once I lost my patience, I was truly out of control. Sometime during this period I traveled home for a visit with my parents and they were shocked at my appearance. At 290 pounds, they thought I looked like a circus freak, but I loved the thought that I was bizarre looking. My father begged me to give up the bodybuilding but I wouldn't listen.

While I was back in Florida having a great time, all my dealer buddies back home had been arrested. They didn't say anything to me but they had all named me as part of 'the ring.' I was now dealing in Florida, and the cops set my friends up to have me bring a shipment home. My personal habit alone was enormous, around $20,000 per year, not to mention what I brought for them. Subsequently, the cops caught me with an arsenal of steroids. I had absolutely no idea what was going to happen to me. When the list of charges was read, I was looking at almost 20 years of prison time because I also carried a handgun. In hindsight, my behavior seems inconceivable and that's the problem with steroids. You think you are invincible, and it all escalates so gradually that moving from one bad choice to another happens pretty easily. I ended up serving nearly five years in a Federal prison.

What's really crazy is that it would have been easy for me to get steroids in prison but after seeing my father cry as I was led from the courtroom, there was no going back for me. I knew from that moment forward I would never touch another steroid.

Prison is hell. It is an upside down world filled with criminals and crimes ranging from money laundering to murder. You learn to survive, but you can never recover the time that you lose. While I was in prison, I missed nieces and nephews being born, friends getting married, and then my dad got terminally ill and I couldn't be with him. The thought of him dying in my absence was devastating.

Following my release, I needed to answer for myself whether or not I was ever really a bodybuilder or just a drug addict taking steroids. I entered a drug-tested bodybuilding contest and did very well. I have done several since. I also wanted to do something to make amends to my community. I decided that talking to kids about my experience with steroids would be the best thing that I could do. The public is so clueless about steroids. There are athletes like John McEnroe, who only took small amounts, and was only exposed by his wife, Tatum O'Neal, after his career was over. Swimmers, track athletes, gymnasts, and soccer players take them. Their bodies may not bulk up but not all steroids do that; they are _performance_ enhancing drugs, not necessarily bulking drugs. Even baseball players like Mark McGuire and Barry Bonds who set tainted Hall of Fame records, all to the joy and accolade of the fans, took them. Are these the right role models for our kids? Is it only cheating if you get caught?

I want to educate people about the easily disguised dangers of this drug. I was an average middle-class kid who loved sports and got sucked down a very dangerous hole. I ask all parents – especially those with children in sports – to educate yourselves about steroids and all performance enhancement drugs. It's not always the top athletes who take steroids; more often it's the average kid who thinks steroids will make him great.

The National Institute on Drug Use and the National Institutes of Health (NIH) report that anabolic steroid use is associated with higher risks of heart attack, stroke and liver disease. The NIH also reports that steroid users who share needles or any devices that are not sterile are at risk of dangerous infections, such as HIV/AIDS, hepatitis B and C, and bacterial endocarditis.

Steroid use often leads to irrational and violent behavior. When it escalates to violence, it's no longer a victimless crime. It's a horrible lie for people to think that they aren't hurting anyone else by doing drugs.

In the case of football great Lyle Alzado, steroids led to violence and early death. Lyle Alzedo was a star defensive end in the NFL. Now he is better remembered for steroid use and his violent temper. Lyle started his drug use in college in 1969, and he was never able to beat it. In 1991, after being diagnosed with brain cancer, he admitted to his steroid use in an issue of *Sports Illustrated.* By 1992 he was dead. The violence spilled over from the playing field to his home, to episodes in public where he would verbally attack people for no reason. He said of his need to take steroids: "I was so wild about winning. It's all I cared about - winning, winning. I never talked about anything else."

Learn more about steroids. Watch for signs. Talk to your children. Tell them about the consequences of buying and taking illegal drugs. Beyond the grotesque physical changes and the rage, the great danger of contracting AIDS or hepatitis is life threatening. Illegal drugs are not regulated or tested. You never know what you're taking. It could be laced with something even more harmful than the steroid.

The most tragic of all side effects are the severe depression and mood swings that often come after stopping steroid use. Too many young athletes have taken their own lives after coming off steroids.

Get familiar with the legal and fringe drugs that are readily available to your student-athletes. Ask them what they are taking and why they are taking it. Read labels. Ask your children's coaches and trainers what their policy is on performance enhancement drugs, supplements and vitamins.

Coach Kirk Ferentz – Iowa Hawkeyes NCAA Division I Football

If you don't think you could ever experience a problem with steroids, then you are probably going to have a problem. If coaches dismiss the subject or just say that they don't have a problem, be alert. There are stories that can break your heart, and they are preventable. Since the NFL has implemented an anti-steroid policy, it will be easier for colleges and high schools to do the same, but coaches and parents have to be proactive.

It's wise to bring in experts and have them talk to the players about the dangers and tell stories about high school and college athletes who have ruined their health and their careers taking steroids.

STEROID NAMES AND USAGE

Pay attention to the news. There are always new drugs coming on the market that have not been widely publicized. Often these aren't covered in drug tests. In 2005 a new and previously undetectable growth hormone THG (tetrahydrogestrinone) hit the news when BALCO, a San Francisco area sports nutrition center was raided. Many big name professional athletes are linked to BALCO. Some may face charges of purchasing THG. The NCAA now tests college athletes for THG and list it as a banned drug.

Some harmful drugs are unregulated and easily available over the internet and in retail stores. They come under the guise of nutritional supplements. These include androstenedione (andro), creatine and ephedra. According to the Blue Cross and Blue Shield Association's Healthy Competition Foundation, these drugs have been reported to cause harmful effects including cramping, headaches and kidney problems. Source: www.healthycompetition.org.

According to the Hormone Foundation, since 1996, children's use of steroids has increased 39% among 8th graders, 67% among 10th graders and 84% among seniors in high school. Source: www.hormone.org

Steroids can be taken in pill form or injected by hypodermic needles directly into muscles. Needle use is as serious a danger as the drug itself. Serious steroid users do something called *stacking*. In this they combine different types of steroids. They also practice *pyramiding*, a method of regulating dosage to get the greatest perceived benefit. There are many different kinds of steroids. The most common anabolic steroids taken today include anadrol, oxandrin, dianabol, winstrol, deca-durabolin and equipoise. Street or slang names for steroids include – gear, roids, juice. Source: www.hormone.org

Football Coach Joe Paterno, Pennsylvania State University

We work very hard to keep steroids out of our program. I have alerted our doctors and trainers that if there is anything that looks unusual, I want to know right away, and we test frequently and randomly for recreational drugs as well. It doesn't mean that it doesn't slip through but we do our best. I was reminded by one of my coaches that I confronted a player, who was a very good player, about his steroid use and he denied he was using. I gave the kid such a hard time he left our program. I am very serious about the subject.

VIOLENCE

"I had a license to kill for 60 minutes a week. My op-
ponents were all fair game and when I got off the field,
I had no regrets. It was like going totally insane."
~ Alex Karras
Winning is Everything and other
American Myths

We live in a culture of violence. Just turn on the television. We've become desensitized to violence. Sports are not an antidote; in fact, it's a place where violence is often condoned. In recent years violence has spilled over from the game, into the stands and locker rooms. It's not just between athletes on and off the field, but also between parents and coaches and athletes and fans. It's every-where. An extreme example of violence between student-athletes occurred in Palmdale, Florida during a youth league baseball game. A 13-year-old player killed a 15-year-old player with a baseball bat. Harry Edwards, a sociology professor at the University of California at Berkeley, said of the killing, "We are developing insensitivity to incivility that increasingly recognizes no bounds as to what we feel we can do if provoked. You see it in road rage. You see it happening in schools. You most certainly see it in athletics, both in the stands and on the field."

Talk to your children about the consequences of violence. Is it worth it to be violent towards an opponent on the field?

What are the consequences of violent behavior?
Physical disabilities, jail time, death

Violence happens because we let it happen. The only way to stop it is through zero tolerance on the part of parents, coaches and athletes. Rules must be communicated and consequences must be immediate and consistent.

Timmy Dance
My Nightmare

We were in Buffalo and we had just won the biggest football game of the season. We were all feeling really good and went out to celebrate. I wasn't 21 yet, so I shouldn't have been drinking to begin with, but we were in a bar and I'd had a few drinks. Some guys at the bar started shoving me, and me being a 'bad' football player and with us having just won our big game, I shoved back. We got into a fight and I hit him and hurt him pretty badly. I didn't realize at the time just how badly. I was arrested and thrown in jail. The first person I called was my grandmother. I was terrified of telling my father and my coach what had happened.

I got out of jail, and after a few weeks I got a letter from the court and learned that I was facing 12 – 15 years in jail for assault. I was suspended from the football team for the rest of the season, and I didn't know if my scholarship was going to be revoked. The worst thing was telling my little brother that I might have to go to jail. I was told to get the best possible legal advice, and, thank God, my father stood by me and found the best lawyers. Each one told me that this situation was very serious. No one reassured us. My father called me eight times a day which scared me even more. I could barely handle one night in jail; I didn't know if I could survive prison. If everybody spent a night in jail, believe me, they would think before they did something wrong. After going to court seven times and mounting up huge legal fees, I was able to plead to a misdemeanor. I got community service and probation for three years.

Looking back, I understand where athletes get their aggression and why they take it off the field. But you can't do that.

There are serious consequences and not just personal ones; the worst part of the experience was what I did to my family.

Hazing

Hazing is considered by some to be an exercise in character building, but it often has irreparable physical and psychological consequences. Methods of hazing include humiliation and violent acts between student-athletes. Because of the embarrassment, victims of hazing are often unwilling to talk about what has happened. Fear and intimidation often keep them from speaking out.

Ask your child's coaches what their policy is on hazing. If it isn't zero tolerance, ask more questions. Ask if there have been incidents in the past. Penn State football coach Joe Paterno believes that hazing is tradition-based. If a school has allowed it in the past, it's tough for a coach to eliminate it. He says that there has to be a zero tolerance policy. You must have consequences right up the line. Coaches, school administrators, school boards and regional and state athletic program directors must communicate consequences. They must take immediate action in any case of hazing. A school superintendent in Utah made the tough decision to take his football team out of the state playoffs in response to a hazing incident. He punished the entire team and sent a strong message to future football players.

College Football Coach Barry Alvarez – Wisconsin Badgers

The only time we see a little hazing is during training camp, and even though it's minor stuff we put a stop to it immediately and punish the older guys. We also lecture them and we let them know what the consequences are. We just don't tolerate hazing.

Some of the worst cases of hazing take place at summer camps. Coaches and trainers are not always aware of what goes on in the bunks at night. The following are examples of publicly reported high school hazing tactics and injuries resulting from them:

- 'Tea bagging' - when a child is held down and the attacker drags or slaps his testicles across the victim's face.

- Broken bones and brain damage resulting from beatings by sticks, paddles, weight belts, bats.

- Concussions caused by "The A Line" where athletes are hit in the head with a hard object wrapped in socks.

- Forcing students to eat excrement, hot peppers and dangerous substances.

- Sexual assaults, forced alcohol intake, "red belly" spankings where the victim is repeatedly slapped on the stomach.

- Forcing kids to run while being shot at with paint balls or bb guns at close range.

Some people continue to see hazing as nothing more than a prank, indoctrination and good fun. The proven truth is that hazing divides schools and towns. It results in law suits, academic suspensions and loss of scholarship money. It leads to injury, psychological damage and death.

Norman J. Pollard, an Alfred University professor who has co-authored two studies on hazing, found that the practice is common not only among high school athletes, but also in every activity from cheerleading to church groups. Hazing happens to students of any age.

"The males tend to use more dangerous and potentially violent acts of hazing, whereas females tend to use humiliation and degradation," Pollard said. "But it is seemingly more and more common, or at least people are coming out into the open about it more frequently."

School districts are taking action against hazing and bullying with specially trained counselors and educational programs. High schools and colleges are making efforts to promote positive rituals and team-building events.

KNOW YOUR CHILDREN'S COACHES

Nowhere is the partnership of the athlete, parent and coach more important than when it comes to educating our children about these challenges and teaching them to overcome their failures.

Parents and coaches must have a zero tolerance policy when it comes to anything that is going to injure or undermine a student-athlete's success. Coaches who condone hazing or drug use are hurting your children. Ask yourself right now: How, as a parent, can you put winning before the health and well being of your flesh and blood? How can coaches put your child at risk for the sake of winning?

Until your children go off to college, you can observe coaches first hand. You can get to know them before the season, off the field. But when your children go to college, they are on their own. It will be up to your children to report any problems that they experience. Before your children pick colleges, research the coaching staff. When you and your children are looking at schools, ask about the following:

- Do they have drug/alcohol educational programs for student-athletes?

- Does the athletic department have a similar program for coaches and staff?

- What is the school's policy on tobacco use?

- What are the guidelines on ergogenic supplement use?

- Will they provide you with a copy of the banned substance policy?

As a parent you should establish a relationship with your children so they know if they've made a mistake, they can come to you. You can deal with it together and start the healing process.

**When guilt rears its ugly head confront it; discuss it
and let go. The past is over. It is time to ask what can
we do right, not what did we do wrong?
Forgive yourself and move on.
Have the courage to reach out for help.**
~ Bernie S. Siegel MD

Ted talks with his sons often about the darker side of sports

Chapter Nine

Recruiting

Twenty years from now you will be more disappointed by the things that you didn't do than by the ones you did do. So throw off the bowlines. Sail away from the safe harbor. Catch the trade winds in your sails. Explore. Dream. Discover.
~ Mark Twain

Countless parents have told me that their children are 'going for' an athletic scholarship, to pay for college. But when I ask *how* they are going about it I'm usually told that when the time comes, the offers will surely come in. But it just doesn't work that way. Pursuing an athletic scholarship has to be a proactive team effort between you, your student-athlete and a coach or trainer. You will need to work together to get the best scholarship offers. Your student's job is to keep up their grades and their level of competition. Your job will include some administrative work or you can hire a service to do it for you. You'll also have to work with your children's coaches to make sure that they are supportive of the effort and will promote your children to college recruiters. If a few different coaches are involved, work with the one who is going to be the most helpful. He or she doesn't necessarily have to be a school coach. You may choose to work with a special trainer or travel team coach. If for any reason, a coach is not supportive, make sure he or she won't stand in the way or negatively impact the process. The recruiting process doesn't have to be overwhelming or complicated. Just get organized and take it one step at a time.

Marva Morris, Mother of Twins - Katina and Cathryn, Marshall College Division I Track Team

My two girls, twins Katina and Cathryn were outstanding track stars in high school, but we knew early on that unless you are a 'super, super' star, colleges aren't going to come find you. You have to go out and find the college that's right for your child. My girls are like night and day. Cathy is a high honors student and an excellent athlete; she is very formal and a true type A personality. Tina is like the wind; she is an honors student and an outstanding athlete – usually taking first to Cathy's second in competition. As different as they are, they decided to go to the same college and hold out for a school that would take them both on scholarship. I supported their decision right from the start.

The girls did most of their research online and they were directly recruited by several state schools in Pennsylvania. They also looked at schools in surrounding states where we had family. We realized early in the process that one of their coaches wasn't supporting their efforts. Katina and Cathryn had turned to another coach to get some extra training and it didn't sit well with him. We didn't let it get in the way. We made the initial phone calls to recruiters and promoted the girls based on their academic and athletic achievements.

Cathy and Tina had seven official visits and Cathy got a full ride scholarship to Fordham, but Tina did not get an offer, so Cathy turned them down. A coach at the University of Buffalo, who already had a full plate with potential recruits, introduced the girls to a coach at Marshall College in West Virginia. It was a great match and now they are both on the Marshall College Thundering Herd Track Team. The academic programs that they chose, Accounting/Pre-Law and Sports Medicine, were very important to their decision. It was the right fit and they are both doing very well.

Mrs. Morris was savvy to the warning signs that her girls' coach was not behind them. Coaches have personal and professional motivations that may not go along with your children's plans. Coaches have a finite amount of resources and time constraints. But there is no reason for that to get in your way. Focus on promoting your students' abilities, grades and personal character. Let the college recruiters decide if your student-athletes have what it takes. The recruiting experience can hold many lessons for student-athletes in negotiating and understanding personal and professional motivations.

THE RECRUITMENT PROCESS

Student-athletes and parents should start thinking about the recruiting process as early as freshman year of high school, and student-athletes should have made a serious commitment to their sport as early as 7th or 8th grade. There are eligibility rules that apply to an athlete's career as early as 9th grade. Rules cover amateurism, drug use, conduct, academic standards and more. One legal infraction or paid athletic event and your children could find themselves ineligible. You don't want to make the mistake of losing eligibility before you even start the application process. Refer to the NCAA (National Collegiate Athletic Association – http://www.ncaa.org), NAIA (National Athletic Intercollegiate Association – http://www.naia.org) and NJCAA (National Junior College Athletic Association – http://njcaa.org) websites. Early research will save you time and possible regrets later on. Don't think for a minute that your children's coaches are going to do all the work. It's up to you to educate yourself about the organizations and the process.

From the time your children start organized team play, you can keep win-loss records, personal achievements and training notes. I've included a journal at the end of this book that you can start using at any stage of your child's athletic career. Once your children are in high school and get serious about pursuing college scholarships, use the notebook for tracking the information you will need on a sports resume and for recruitment interviews. Encourage your student-athletes to track their own progress and take ownership of their bid for a scholarship. Let them take the lead whenever possible. This is a big step in their lives. They will need support and guidance, but I don't think that parents and coaches should dictate the process.

Dorothy Kerner, Mother of Student-athlete Erin Kerner, College Basketball Player

Erin started playing basketball in 2nd grade. By 3rd grade she started intramurals and was showing some talent. We were shocked at her outstanding dribbling skills. We tried very hard not to push her, but we supported her in all the steps that she wanted to take in the sport and always stressed academics and good behavior. We wanted her to respect her teammates and coaches.

Erin progressed in the sport and moved on to traveling teams. We let her play as long as she kept up her grades, and by her junior year she was inducted into the National Honor Society with a 3.9 grade point average.

Before we knew it, it was time to look at colleges. I think she was very smart about how she approached the recruiting process. We visited four of the colleges that made her an offer and met with the coaches. She even got to play with some of the basketball teams. She paid very close attention to the academic programs. Erin chose Quinnipiac University for its business school and the atmosphere. They went out of their way to make us feel comfortable. We met everyone from the president of the university to the dean of the business school to the coaches and even the janitorial staff. They let it be understood throughout the process that they are dedicated to putting education first.

As a mother I was very impressed with how Erin approached the recruiting process. I think you have to let your children take the lead but be there for guidance when they need it.

I can't stress enough the importance of academics. Your student-athletes must put their grades first in high school to be considered for a scholarship, and then keep their grades up in college to keep their scholarship.

Recruiting typically starts during your student-athlete's junior year. Colleges and universities that have taken an interest in your sons or daughters will start contacting their school by phone or letter. Your son or daughter may also begin to receive several interest letters directly.

Recommended steps in the recruiting process.
- Learn About the Collegiate Athletic Organizations
- Understand Eligibility and Probabilities
- Determine Roles and Responsibilities
- Prepare Your Athletic Resume
- Prepare Your Videos/Highlight Films
- Plan Your Tournament Schedule
- Select Potential Colleges and Make Contact
- Prepare for Your First Meeting with a Recruiter
- Plan Your College Visits
- Choose the *Right* School

THE ORGANIZATIONS

THE NCAA

The NCAA (National Collegiate Athletic Association), considered by many to represent the highest level of college sports, has three Divisions with Division 1-A being the best of the best. The NCAA oversees approximately 88 championships in 23 sports. The NCAA also oversees several club sports that do not have championships. More than 40,000 student-athletes compete in NCAA championships each year. A first step in getting to know the NCAA should be a visit to the website and, in particular, to their Athletic Eligibility Clearinghouse page where you can learn about basic requirements including academics, standardized test scores, recommendations, proof of amateur status and rules concerning sports betting and drug use violations.

NCAA Statement of Purpose: "Our purpose is to govern competition in a fair, safe, equitable and sportsmanlike manner and to integrate intercollegiate athletics into higher education so that the educational experience of the student-athlete is paramount." Source: http://ncaa.org

The NCAA has three Divisions. NCAA Division I is considered the top college sports level. Division II ranks below Division I and generally offers fewer scholarships, and in Division III offers no athletic grants in aid, but other forms of financial aid are sometimes awarded.

Colleges cannot be members of both the NCAA and NAIA and choose which organization to join based on a number of factors including size of school, athletic budget, and athletic ability. There is also the NJCAA - National Junior College Athletic Association, similar to the other two organizations but governing Junior College Athletics.

NCAA Championship sports include:

MEN: Baseball, Basketball, Cross Country, Fencing, Football, Golf, Gymnastics, Ice Hockey, Lacrosse, Rifle, Skiing, Soccer, Swimming, Tennis, Track and Field, Volleyball, Water Polo and Wrestling.

WOMEN: Archery, Badminton, Basketball, Bowling, Cross Country, Equestrian, Fencing, Field Hockey, Golf, Gymnastics, Lacrosse, Rowing, Skiing, Soccer, Softball, Squash, Swimming, Synchronized Swimming, Team Handball, Tennis, Volleyball and Water Polo.

THE NAIA (NATIONAL ASSOCIATION OF INTERCOLLEGIATE ATHLETES)

The NAIA is also divided into three Divisions, and in general Division I schools can offer more sports scholarships than Division II schools with no athletic scholarships available in Division III. The NAIA is more broad-based than the NCAA and has schools ranging from a few hundred students to over 10,000. Please do not listen to those who say that this association is second best to the NCAA. Your children's futures are based on the best college fit, and that might mean a smaller school or an NAIA scholarship where they can excel in sports and academics and get the best out of their college years. Look for the best academic and social fit for your children, so they feel comfortable and will be more likely to carry the additional burden of a team sport. The NAIA Divisions are competitive with NCAA in almost all sports except Division I Football.

The NAIA has a **Champions of Character** initiative intended to create an environment in which every NAIA student-athlete, coach, official and spectator is committed to the true spirit of competition through respect, integrity, responsibility, leadership and sportsmanship.

NAIA: Statement of Purpose: "A Code of Ethics is the essential tool with which to protect and promote the interests of athletics and the coaching profession. Its primary purpose is to clarify and distinguish ethical practices from those which are detrimental and harmful. Its secondary purposes are to emphasize the values of athletics in American and Canadian educational institutions and to stress the functional contributions of coaches to their schools and players. Ethics must be defined as the basic principles of right action. Proper ethics in athletics implies a standard of character which affords confidence and trust. The standards emphasized in this code certainly rest in the hands of those engaged in the athletics field."

NAIA Championship sports include:

WOMEN: Basketball, Cross Country, Golf, Soccer, Softball, Swimming & Diving, Tennis, Track & Field, Volleyball.

MEN: Baseball, Basketball, Cross Country, Football, Golf, Soccer, Swimming & Diving, Tennis, Track & Field, Wrestling.

Both the NCAA and NAIA have very serious expectations and rules that are strictly enforced. Your student-athletes will be expected to raise their level of self-discipline and conduct if they are awarded a scholarship. These organizations represent something bigger than just your child's college team competition; they are national organizations with great history and the highest standards of conduct. When being considered for a scholarship, your student-athletes will be judged, not just for their athletic ability but for their overall potential as young men and women. No matter how great an athlete your children are, there are going to be hundreds of other athletes just as talented who are going to be vying for the same scholarships. If two potential scholarship recipients have similar skills and ability in competition, then the schools will look at academic standing, character, community service and attitude. This is a time for your children to shine as people, not just as athletes.

ELIGIBILITY AND PROBABILITY

Before you go to the effort of helping your children pursue athletic scholarships, make sure that they are both eligible and understand the difficult odds that are against them. All high-school athletes who want to compete in college must register with the Initial-Eligibility Clearinghouse. The Clearinghouse provides information on how student-athletes comply with NCAA bylaws in order to compete in intercollegiate athletics. It includes information about what high school students need to do in order to be eligible to compete in their first year in college, as well as guidelines that coaches and prospects must follow during the recruiting process. Information is also included on conduct issues that have eligibility ramifications, such as gambling and the use of sports agents. For more information, go to: http://www2.ncaa.org/legislation_and_governance/eligibility_and_conduct/eligibility.htm

A harsh dose of reality is served up on the NCAA website where recruitment probability is reported each year. Student-athletes, coaches and parents should be brutally honest about the tough road ahead. Be realistic and accept the effort for the rewards beyond the scholarship money. Your children are reaching for something big, and if they miss, be happy that they tried. They will be far better off having made the effort than not trying at all.

Coaches must provide athletes and parents with their honest assessment of athletes' potential. Don't put blinders on – listen to the coach's assessment of their chances. Remember that a coaches' reputations rest on their recommendations. Coaches can't recommend athletes who are not particularly talented and still get respect from the recruiting community. But, as previously stated, be aware that coaches may not have the time to promote your student-athletes, in which case you should look for another coach or trainer to provide a recommendation or go it alone.

Mike Mischler, Former Head Football Coach at Cathedral Prep in Erie, Pennsylvania
Selected AFM's Schutt Sports National High School Coach of the Year in 2000, Mischler sent over 75 of his players on to play college football at all levels in a seven year career. He resigned from his position in January 2005

It's important for parents, coaches and athletes to work together during the recruiting process. Parents should talk with coaches early on – even during freshman year—to become knowledgeable about the program and learn about the methods the coaches use to get athletes recruited. It's natural for all parents to want a full scholarship for their children. Coaches have to be more objective. Their credibility with college recruiters is on the line.

Coaches play a big role in the recruiting process. The coach has a role to market the child to the various national recruiting lists that are out there – it's never too early to get a player's name circulated in the recruiting system. Get their names out freshmen year; colleges don't recruit that young, but it's important to get on as many lists as possible.

The coaches can open and close doors, depending on their evaluation of students' ability and character, to college recruiters. Coaches must give an honest evaluation of each athlete because recruiters actually rate high school coaches on their performance in that area. If coaches misrepresent athletes to a school, their future evaluations will have no merit.

Most importantly, I have to underscore the importance of academics – parents need to make sure that school work gets done every night! Oftentimes, it is the freshmen and sophomore year grades that most affect the "recruitability" of players.

After you talk with the coaches and trainers, talk with your children about their chances. Parents have to take a long hard look in the mirror and make the decision whether or not to encourage their children to go for scholarships.

NCAA DATA ON PROBABILITY OF COLLEGE RECRUITMENT

Student athletes	Men's Basketball	Women's Basketball	Football	Baseball	Men's Ice Hockey	Men's Soccer
High School Student-athletes	549,500	456,900	983,600	455,300	29,900	321,400
High School Senior Student-athletes	157,000	130,500	281,000	130,100	8,500	91,800
NCAA Student-athletes	15,700	4,400	56,500	25,700	3,700	8,200
NCAA Freshman Roster Positions	4,500	4,100	6,200	7,300	1,100	5,200
NCAA Senior Student-athletes	3,500	3,200	12,600	5,700	800	4,100
NCAA Student-athletes Drafted	44	32	250	600	33	76
Percent High School to NCAA	2.9	3.1	5.8	5.6	12.9	5.7
Percent NCAA to Professional	1.3	1.0	2.0	10.5	4.1	1.9
Percent High School to Professional	0.03	0.02	0.09	0.5	0.4	0.08

Source: http://www.ncaa.org/research/prob_of_competing/
Note: These percentages are based on estimated data and should be considered approximations of the actual percentages. Data is from 2003

While the most popular sports present some tough odds, there are less popular sports such as golf, fencing and diving with a more favorable ratio of students to scholarships. Not all athletic scholarships are full-ride like football and basketball. These are so called "head count sports". Most of these are classed as equivalency sports, like golf or fencing or diving. This means that coaches can share their scholarship allocation among a group of students. This is not a bad thing. Partial scholarships are better than no scholarship and may open doors for academic scholarship considerations. If you have *A* students who can break 85 on the golf course, they may get a reduction on their college tuitions and have a great experience traveling on college sports teams. Part of the college athletes' experiences are seeing the country or the world and meeting new people. A sport like rowing may not pay 'full boat' but may take the student to England for a few weeks of competition and fun. Look beyond the money; athletics can open wonderful new doors for your students.

OTHER NCAA SPORTS:
GOLF

There are about 289 Division I and 186 Division II colleges that offer men's golf scholarships and about 217 Division I and 90 Division II colleges that offer scholarships for women, for a total of 1,970 men's golf scholarships and 1,788 for women. If your children can consistently beat a score of 85, they can start thinking seriously about a college golf scholarship.

TRACK AND FIELD

There are approximately 271 Division I and 148 Division II colleges that offer track and field scholarships for men. For women there are 290 Division I and 108 Division II colleges that offer Indoor track and field scholarships.

TENNIS

Women's tennis is classed as a "head count" sport which means that the scholarships that are offered are full-ride scholarships. Men's tennis, on the other hand, is classed as an equivalency sport which means that coaches can share the scholarship allocation among a greater number of players.

There are 274 Division I and 164 Division II colleges that offer tennis scholarships for men. For women there are 316 Division II and Division II colleges that offer financial aid for tennis. That's a total of 1,971 men's tennis scholarships available in the NCAA alone and for women's tennis there are 3,794 scholarships.

Determine Roles and Responsibilities

Now that you understand the odds and decided to help your child pursue a scholarship, it's time to get organized. Decide who is going to do what. Don't count on colleges seeking out your student-athletes or high school coaches doing all the work for you. Here is a story of one father who treated the process like a business and got the job done.

A Recruitment Story - Jeffery Johnson - Father

Not living in the same town as my son, sports took on a special significance for us. It was our time to bond and spend time together. I traveled to every game, no matter where it was. My son Jeff was an exceptional football player in high school, and, as a running back from California, he had a unique and specific talent that I knew would attract attention. I had no doubt that he was college material, but he wasn't getting any recruiting letters. I used the lack of attention to show him that you have to go out and find your opportunities in life. I decided not to use a marketing agency for him and just do it myself. I contacted over 100 schools in the NAIA and Division I programs and sent out 85 tapes, and he got 13 offers. I was told that the coaches appreciated hearing directly from the family and not from an agent. I think it took me about 100 to 150 hours, but, with some organization, setting up a spreadsheet and communicating through email whenever possible, it really didn't seem like an overwhelming task.

I recommend that parents point out in their first communication that *they are the parent* of the child, if it isn't obvious. I also recommend showing statistics right up front along with academic standing and community service. You want the coaches to know that you have responsible children who will keep up their grades. While your goal is to get a tape in the school's hands, recruiters won't request one unless you get the right statistics in front of them at the start such as your athletes' speed, physical stature, weight, and vertical leap. If you put in the work, you'll get results.

Recruiting Services

There is a lot of controversy regarding recruitment services. Some college coaches say that they want to hear directly from the student and parents because they don't like the manufactured approach of the commercial agencies. But if you are a parent who simply doesn't have the time, I recommend finding a recruitment service to do the work, but one that will stay behind the scenes. All communications to coaches should look like they are coming directly from you. Do not use a service that insists on using its letterhead. You want all communications coming from you – not them.

Mike and Ken Lancaster operate Athletic Scholarship Sports Recruiting Service, www.athleticscholarships.net, which offers professional resume and recruiting services and covers all NCAA and NAIA sports. They prepare an athletic profile or resume on your behalf and forward it to every college coach in the United States. Look for a service like the Lancasters' where resumes are sent out on your letterhead, not theirs, and initial advice and assessment are free of charge. When looking for a service, ask questions about the accuracy of its college database.

Ken's advice is to be very careful when choosing a recruiting service. There are many out there, but some are not worth the money. Do not be conned by flashy websites. Also remember that there is little point in having an athletic resume posted on a recruiting service website. Coaches rarely surf the Internet for prospective athletes.

Finally, beware of any recruiting service that promises to get you a scholarship or tells you that it knows the secrets to getting a scholarship. THERE ARE NO SECRETS AND THERE ARE NO GUARANTEES. Please note: all recruiting services are independent companies and in no way affiliated with this book. Parents, student-athletes, and readers should use their own discretion in choosing any services related to the recruiting process.

The Resume

Next, you need a strong resume for your student-athlete. Most Division I, II and III colleges have never heard of your children or seen them play, so it is imperative that your athletes build a resume that includes facts and personal achievements in their sports. Include academics, community service and special honors. Many great young athletes are overlooked because their resumes aren't well written or they neglect to prepare one at all. Keep your options open regarding the size and division of the school so that you have a variety from which to choose. There are more than 600 colleges across the nation offering sports scholarships. Your children's resumes should include details such as sports achievements, special honors, strength, speed, academic achievements, and community service.

Sample Resume:

Thomas S. Dance
Current Grade: Senior (12th) E-mail: tom@sports.net
Address: 502 West 5th St,
Erie, PA 16502 Phone: (814) 000-0000

Current School: Cathedral Preparatory School
225 West 9th Street Erie, PA 16501
Height: 6'2"   Weight: 195   Jersey No: 8

Offensive Position: Wide Out/ Quarter Back Preferred
Position: Wide Out
Defensive Position: Free Safety
100 Meter Dash: 10.67
Bench: 240x 8 Reps./Squats:505x 8 Reps.

GPA. 3.4 Athletic Honors:
1. Won 2003 110 Hurdle State Championship (1st Place)
2. Presently holds school record for 110m hurdles
Old Record: 14.7
New Record: 14.4 (Tom Dance)
Hand Held Time: 13.7
3. Awarded the 2003 <u>McDowell Invitational Most Outstanding Track Athlete.</u>
Individual Events: (1st in the 110 hurdles) (1st in the 100 meter yard dash)

4.   2002-2003 All Metro Hurdler and Sprinter.

State Qualifier sophomore year in the 110 hurdles, Track and Field Varsity Letters, Football Varsity Letters, Times News Athlete of the Week, All Metro Football Team.

Coach: Michael Mischler
Home Phone: (814)000-0000
Work Phone: (814) 000-0000 ext. 224

Recruiters like resumes on plain white paper in plain white envelopes. There is no reason to get fancy with flashy stationery. Let your students' stats do the talking. Get your students' resumes together and have them ready for mail or email.

Highlight Films

Nothing will have the impact of a video of your student-athletes in action. After sending resumes and making initial contacts, your goal is to get a tape in the recruiters' hands. Many high schools across the nation make films and can have them readily available for you. Talk to your childrens' coaching staffs to confirm that they are catching your student-athletes on film or take the initiative and do the filming yourself. Build a collection of films of their events or games. Have copies on hand when recruiters request a tape.

> **It's not the size of the dog in the fight,**
> **It's the size of the fight in the dog.**
> ~ *Dwight D. Eisenhower*

Plan Your Tournament Schedule

At some point during the recruiting process, recruiters will want to see students perform if they have not already done so. If your children's seasons are in, you may want to contact your recruiting coaches and give them a list of game dates. By now, you would have already sent them highlight films, which in most cases will be enough. In the case of my son Tommy, his scholarship could have been in either track or football. He chose football. On tape, the coaches could see he had speed just from watching him out-run the opposing team, but the coaches couldn't see how fast the opposing team members were. We sent the colleges a resume with his best times recorded, but unfortunately some recruits fudge their times. The Iowa Hawkeyes recruiting coach for our area had a lot of interest in Tommy, so he came to a track meet to see just how fast he was. Purdue University was particularly interested in Tommy's time in the 100 meters and asked for proof prior to making an offer. We scanned a newspaper clipping and emailed it to confirm that he actually did have the speed we said he had. Be prepared to back up your athletes' stats. Use press coverage and invite recruiters to competitions.

SELECT POTENTIAL COLLEGES AND MAKE CONTACT

Now you have your students' resumes, highlight films and tournament schedules together. It's time for your student to pick the colleges they want to pursue. Oftentimes, this process can be the most difficult step. The decision goes way beyond the money being offered. You must consider factors related to colleges such as academic offerings, geographic location, and campus environment. It's important to begin narrowing choices right away. Start by helping your children align the academic program with their ultimate career goals. If your student-athletes want to pursue engineering, don't look at schools known for their music program, no matter what the scholarship opportunities.

Recruitment consultant Ken Lancaster recommends that students and parents put academics first when considering a college. According to Ken, "The sports program should be secondary unless it is the only way that the student/athlete can earn a college degree. The chances of making a career from playing a sport after college are not great and should not be relied on as a future career. Put the degree first."

Jenifer Trowell, Student-Athlete, Lacrosse, Gannon University

I started playing basketball in middle school. My parents thought that I would stick with the sport, but a coach introduced me to lacrosse and I really liked it. I played it in the off-season just to stay in shape, but then I got serious about lacrosse in my sophomore year. My parents didn't really understand me switching from basketball to lacrosse because they just hadn't been exposed to the sport and it seemed like everyone played basketball.

Getting serious about a new sport wouldn't have been possible without the help of my coach and my school. With the encouragement of my coach, I went to lacrosse camp which is a big step if you want to get recruited. You have to go to the camps where the college coaches are; you have to be seen.

When you are looking for a school, I recommend going online and researching. I wanted to pursue a major in physical therapy, so that was my first criteria. You have to put your academic interests first. Next, I looked at the size of the school I wanted, and then I looked at the lacrosse program. Find your top ten picks and then go visit them, see the games and level of competition at the schools, then contact the coaches and send a film.

Visit the campuses online and get a sense of the environment. Some college campuses are located in urban settings, some rural. Your student-athletes should be comfortable with the environment. It will help them adjust to college life much more easily. If possible, depending on the maturity level of your student-athletes, you may want to consider a college or university that is also close to home. If you help your children find the right fit, they will be more likely to hold on to their scholarships.

At this point, it is very important that your children appreciate the long road ahead of them. Getting a scholarship is just the first step. It will take hard work and dedication to keep up their grades, perform well in their sports, and maintain their scholarships. This is an opportunity of a lifetime and should be respected as such.

Prepare for Your First Meeting with a Recruiter

We called the colleges that my sons were interested in and spoke directly to the recruiting coaches for their sports and, in some cases, a specific position coach such as a wide receiver's coach or quarterback's coach. I am not a fan of emailing alone without a series of phone calls. These coaches get thousands of emails every month, and yours could get lost in the masses.

We prepared a list of questions concerning academics, rules for incoming freshman, living quarters, tutoring options for athletes if needed, and other particulars. We also inquired about the average GPA of the team. Beware, if the average GPA of team member's is low, there is a great risk of many of your starters becoming ineligible which will affect the team. Also, find out what the graduation rate is for student-athletes. You may also ask how many students the school is recruiting in your child's specific position and how many upper classman they presently have in that position. Keep in mind that just because your children are recruited as wide receivers in football, this doesn't mean they will end up in that position. Many student-athletes end up playing positions other than what they were recruited for or played in high school. My younger son was a quarterback and wide receiver and ended up playing defensive back in college.

Plan Your College Visits

When planning your college visits, make sure your children are well rested and ready for a very long day of interviews and touring. Your children will be assigned to student-athletes at the school who will show them around. Talk with your children about the fact that they are making a big decision that will affect the next four years of their lives, based on this one visit. Encourage them to get the most out of the visit and ask questions. If you go along on the tour, ask the college athletes about their opinions of the school and the sports program but beware, the student-athletes who are showing you around typically play the same position that your children hope to play. The college athletes may be motivated to discourage your children to avoid some fresh competition the next year.

Don't be distracted by Division I, II or III designations. Instead, focus on academic programs. Your children's educations should come first when choosing a school. Many young athletes who want to pursue a professional career in sports are afraid that a Division II or III school will not provide a chance at going pro. This is not true. Many of our nation's greatest athletes attended Division II and III colleges.

Athletes transfer from one college to another for various reasons; however, there is a drawback to transferring between Division I-A colleges. These athletes will lose a year of eligibility. They must transfer to another Division in order to maintain continuous play eligibility. Review the policy on credit transfers at any school you consider. It's possible that your children could lose some credits, depending on the college. I don't recommend transferring more than once if at all possible. Multiple transfers could have an adverse effect on your students' academic programs.

After my son Timmy attended two years at a Division I-A school, he discovered it was not a good fit for him. He transferred to a Division II school to continue his education and athletic career. There he received a combination of scholarship money, grants and loans. Before making the transfer, we notified many Division I-AA and Division II and III schools of his decision. Many schools were interested in offering him a full scholarship, but he made sure that he based his choice on the best environment, not the best scholarship offer.

Tommy Dance
Recruiting Experience

I began to establish my goals during my freshman year of high school. My initial goal was to start on the freshman football team. I was immediately moved up to the junior varsity team, and, for the first time in my life, I realized that hard work really does pay off.

After experiencing a great junior varsity season, it was time to start track for the first season. I was a little apprehensive because I wasn't sure what events I could run, and I knew the competition was going to be stiff. In searching for an event, I gravitated to the areas where the team needed the most help. After completing my search, I became a hurdler. I had never hurdled before in my life so I knew it was going to take a lot of hard work in addition to regular practice.

This is when having a father who wanted me to succeed came into play. It started simply by him taking me to the gym to lift weights before practice and to the local track to run after practice. It was hard in the beginning because none of my close friends wanted to put in the extra work that would make them better athletes.

Sophomore year was another solid year for football. I was starting quarterback on the junior varsity team and seeing action on the varsity team. I knew the upcoming track season would have potential for me because of the hard work I had put in the year before. The season ended with an opportunity for me to participate in the State Track Meet. My experience was cut short in the semifinals when I lost my heat by .001 seconds. After the disappointment that I experienced at States, I realized that I never wanted that feeling again. When I returned home, my father and I trained twice as hard for next season.

Junior year arrived, and it was time for summer football already. During drills I noticed that I was bigger, stronger, and faster than I had been the year before. During football camp it was apparent I had a good chance at becoming a starter. The starting role was very important to me because junior year is a crucial time in the recruiting process. When Division I colleges began showing interest in me, the only questions they were posing concerned my speed.

To put all of their concerns to rest, I chose the upcoming track season to show them just how fast I was. The first obstacle I had to overcome was when the Iowa Hawkeye recruiting coach came to watch me run. I knew what he was there for, so I showed him what he wanted to see. My next goal was to compete well at the State track meet because I knew a lot of coaches would be there. I advanced past the qualifying rounds to a spot in the finals. Although I was not top seed, and the odds were stacked against me, I won the state championship. Standing at the top of the award podium made me realize that all the hard work had paid off.

During the summer before my senior year, I made unofficial visits to colleges that had been corresponding with me. Having both my father and my brother along helped me feel more comfortable with my decision making. During a lot of these visits the coaches did something called an "eye" test where they take a look at you physically to see if you are able to play at the next level.

Soon after I got home, I started receiving phone calls from colleges. Then I received multiple full scholarship offers from Division I schools. My dad and I started to evaluate what schools offered the best combination of academics, football and environment. I knew that Michigan State was the best choice for me. It had a good football team in the Big Ten Conference, was close to home, had a coaching staff that I got along well with, and, most importantly, offered a good education. My Dad was happy with my choice because I had taken the time to look at each school before making my decision. Before athletes decide what school to go to, they should visit the ones they're interested in, so they know they've made the right choice.

I gave a verbal commitment to MSU at the beginning of my senior year, giving the head coach my commitment to sign with their University on signing day. I had a great senior football and track season. In football we were one game away from making it to States, which was a lot better than we had been the year before. In track I was able to repeat as a State champ in the 110-meter high hurdles and then went to compete at the National meet.

As I continue my athletic career, I look back at what it took to get this far, and I realize that it is not an easy process. It takes determination and dedication to compete at the next level. It is going to be the extra work you put in at the gym or on the track that separates you from the pack. It all comes down to how badly you want it.

BEYOND THE OFFER

As a parent who has gone through the experience twice, I have a word of warning. Some student-athletes get cocky by senior year when they think their scholarship bid is a sure thing. Remind your athletic stars that their academic standing and their behavior, on and off the field, have to be maintained until high school graduation. Senior year in high school is no time to slack off in academics or sports or, worse, do something stupid to risk their scholarship. I interviewed a man who went down the wrong path when he was younger. His life has turned out for the best, but he wonders where he might be if things had taken a different turn.

Mark

I'm telling my story as a warning to all the cocky young athletes out there who think they are invincible. Just because you are a star on the field doesn't mean that teachers or any adult will give you a pass in the other areas of your life.

I went to a great Catholic prep school in Boston, Massachusetts. I did pretty well in school, but I excelled in baseball. By junior year I was getting attention from colleges and my coach was sure that I would get a scholarship if I kept my nose clean and my grades up. As long as I had baseball, I stayed out of trouble. I had friends who made easy money selling drugs, and sometimes I was tempted to go that route, but baseball kept me from going down the wrong path. That is until disaster struck.

First semester senior year, the principal called me down to his office to give me the most devastating news I could have imagined. He told me that my Spanish teacher had given me a failing grade for the first semester which meant that I wasn't eligible to play baseball. I had lived in Puerto Rico and knew the language but the teacher failed me for my cocky attitude and because I wasn't doing the work.

The principal told me that he had tried to talk her out of it, but she wouldn't budge. He tried to settle me down and told me to take a couple of days off to get myself together. This was the first time I felt as if I couldn't restrain myself. I ran out of

his office, headstrong as ever, and went downstairs to the Spanish teacher's class. I barged in and we had a loud confrontation.
She was unrelenting, and I was angrier than I had ever been
before. I felt like my life was over. I'll never forget that day as
long as I live.

The principal called me a couple of days later and told me
he managed to save me from expulsion, but the teacher needed
to speak to my mother. I didn't even care at that point, but my
mother did go down to the school and then she cried her eyes
out for days.

I rarely showed up for school during the last semester of my
senior year. I graduated, but just barely, and I took some college
classes, but without baseball I had no interest in school. Then I
took the easy route and went down the wrong path - way down.
I got involved with drug dealers and gangsters. I ran from the
law for years. It took me a long time to redeem myself. I'm in
my 30's now and I've come around. I paid my dues and life
is good, but sometimes I wonder about that moment in high
school when things went very wrong. Being cocky and getting
angry doesn't get you anywhere.

I recommend to all parents that they provide consistent support and guidance from junior high right through the recruitment
process. Your children's academic and athletic standards should
remain on an even keel. Take it all one step at a time and talk to
your children about discipline and moderation. Avoid undue pressure and overreaction to disappointments. Great highs and lows and
histrionics lead to crash and burn lifestyles. If your children do make
it to the pros, big paychecks and temporary fame will pose a dangerous lifestyle. It will be their upbringing and your consistent guidance
that will help them maintain a steady and purposeful life.

CHAPTER TEN

LIVING

Ted, Timmy and Tommy

I'm not a professional coach, nor am I a minister, doctor or psychologist; I'm a Dad. For most of my sons' lives, I was a single dad. I think that makes me the most important person in their youth, and that's what qualified me to write this book. I've often thought that people should have to pass a test before having children, but there's no formal training for the most important job in your life. In my case, I had a wonderful mother who taught me well and showed me that I could raise two terrific sons.

Building character in your children benefits everyone. Our children are the next generation of scientists, doctors and business owners. In some cases they are the next professional athletes. Where will we be if we continue to turn out adults who lack character, and who respect and fear nothing? Look at the cheating that takes place in corporate America and in professional sports. We, as parents and professionals, need to set positive examples in everything we do in order to combat this trend.

Youth sports organizations should be safe shelters for children, places where they can learn right from wrong. This isn't always the case. I urge parents to offer support and take action in their children's athletic programs. You can be a positive support for coaches and a helpful guide to other parents. You can also be a support to children other than your own. You can do this by coaching, assisting or helping to introduce a code of conduct into your school or sports program.

Present positive sports role models to your children. Help them set goals and follow through on them. It's never too late. Your greatest legacy will be to teach your children how to raise their own children.

When I was faced with raising two children alone, I turned to God and to my mother. That is where I found the support, the spirit, and the strength. I believe that we help instill the spirit that sees our children through the rest of their lives. If we are positive and kind and encouraging, our children will pass that spirit on to others.

**The fruit of the Spirit is love, joy, peace, patience,
kindness, generosity, faithfulness, gentleness
and self-control.
*~ Galatians 5:22***

As parents we make or break our children's shots at happy, healthy adulthoods. We show them the way, then stand back and let them fend for themselves. Teaching your children to be a true athletic star is one of the best things you can do for them. It doesn't matter if they play college sports or even high school sports. What is important is that you've taught them to have respect for their own health and well being and the well being of others. To be an athletic star is to be a good person who tries hard, plays by the rules and enjoys the game – no matter what game.

I hope you use the journal section in this book, not just to monitor your children's athletic careers, but to enjoy the process and someday to look back on the coaches and moments that helped build your children's character.

Raising my sons was the most important job I ever had. I think I did it pretty well. They are living as true athletic stars, and I hope they will raise their own children in the same way that I did.

Timmy Dance on Raising His Own Children

When the time comes to introduce my children to sports, it will definitely be an emotional day for me. I have learned many life lessons through sports and I truly feel that if my children have the "want to and will" attitude they can also learn from athletics. When the time comes I will stop myself from forcing it on them. Even though I want my children to be athletes, I will always be proud of them no matter what they want to do with their lives, as long as they put maximum effort in doing it. If they choose to be athletes, everything I have learned from my experiences I will pass on to them.

I asked Wade Salem, Area Director of the Fellowship of Christian Athletes, for his advice on how we can all work together to promote character building in youth sports. On a positive note we talked about how we both see a movement towards change. Coaches are starting to value character over flamboyance, aggression and grandstanding. But Wade believes that the problem of coaching to 'win at all cost' is still rampant in youth sports.

Wade Salem, Area Director,
Fellowship of Christian Athletes

The issue is with parents, coaches and our society placing value on outward appearance and performance over the character and inner qualities of an athlete. We tend to value the child who is the big scorer and always has the ball. We don't look at the fact that the big scorers who are also the ones who are so selfish they won't share the ball with anyone else. What are those children going to be like as adults, trying to cope with marriage and a career?

The question is: how do we use the sports experience to develop character in our children? I see parents who are so focused on performance that they forget the inside stuff. I want to encourage them to communicate differently with their children. After a game, instead of saying, "You should have made that shot," what the athletes need to hear is praise and approval for who they are, not just what they do. We should be saying, "I love to watch you play" or "that was a great effort." Then, later after you get home you can say, "Next time why don't you try…"

Encouragement and positive instruction build character. The word "character" comes from the Greek "to scratch" or "engrave". Unfortunately, we have become a society of image focusing on what's superficial on the outside, but that's not what counts in crunch time. We need to help parents, coaches and athletes understand that character development comes from consistent and continuous training. We must create patterns of behavior that create good habits in our children. How are you training your children and what does it look like? Is it just physical? Or are you paying attention to the whole package – body, mind and spirit?

I'm happy to say that character development is making a comeback. Coaches are now asking, "What kind of kid are they?" Character is becoming as important as statistics. If parents can start to heal their own wounded hearts, they will stop wounding their children and other players and start helping their children develop self control, passion in participation and truly grow towards great character.

Parenting is an eighteen-year balancing act performed on a slippery high wire. Parents need all the help they can get. While writing this book, I've learned that there is a lot of help out there. There seems to be a powerful groundswell of support for promoting healthy lifestyles and character development in children. This is clearly a response to the "win at any cost" mentality that has taken over our media and culture. No caring parent wants to give into the dark pressures of cheating, violence, obesity or drug use. Some parents either aren't aware of the problems their children face or they don't know what to do about them. At the end of this book, you'll find a sports journal to track your student athlete's career!

Train up a child in the way he should go,
and when he is old he will not depart from it.
Proverbs 22:6

Timmy Dance

Tommy Dance, Signing Day

SPORTS JOURNAL

SPORTS JOURNAL

SPORTS JOURNAL

SPORTS JOURNAL

SPORTS JOURNAL

SPORTS JOURNAL

SPORTS JOURNAL

SPORTS JOURNAL

SPORTS JOURNAL

SPORTS JOURNAL

SPORTS JOURNAL

SPORTS JOURNAL

SPORTS JOURNAL

SPORTS JOURNAL

SPORTS JOURNAL

SPORTS JOURNAL

SPORTS JOURNAL

SPORTS JOURNAL

SPORTS JOURNAL

SPORTS JOURNAL

SPORTS JOURNAL

SPORTS JOURNAL

SPORTS JOURNAL

SPORTS JOURNAL

SPORTS JOURNAL